Battlefields of
LEICESTERSHIRE

TREVOR HICKMAN

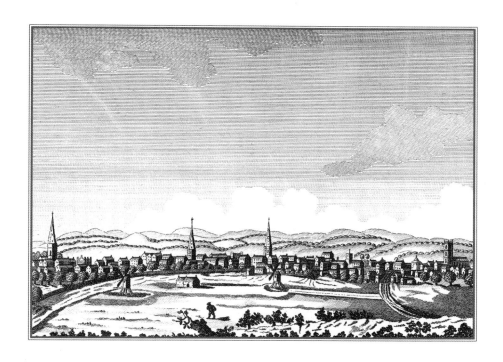

SUTTON PUBLISHING

Sutton Publishing Limited
Phoenix Mill · Thrupp · Stroud
Gloucestershire · GL5 2BU

First published 2004

Title page photograph: An eighteenth-century view of Leicester from the South Fields, featuring the churches of St Mary, St Nicholas, St Martin and St Margaret.

British Library Cataloguing in Publication Data
A catalogue record for this book is available from the British Library.

ISBN 0-7509-3658-4

Typeset in 11/12pt ACaslon Regular.
Typesetting and origination by
Sutton Publishing Limited.
Printed and bound in England by
J.H. Haynes & Co. Ltd, Sparkford.

By the same author

Around Melton Mowbray in Old Photographs
Melton Mowbray in Old Photographs
East of Leicester in Old Photographs
The Melton Mowbray Album
The Vale of Belvoir in Old Photographs
The History of the Melton Mowbray Pork Pie

The History of Stilton Cheese
Melton Mowbray to Oakham
Around Rutland in Old Photographs
Leicestershire Memories
The Best of East Leicestershire & Rutland
The Best of Leicester
The Best of Leicestershire

Ashby de la Zouch Castle, *c.* 1840.

Contents

A south-easterly view of Leicester, *c.* 1820. There are two windmills in the foreground, and the churches of St Nicholas, St Martin, All Saints and St Margaret, and the ruins of Leicester Abbey on the right.

In Memoriam

Of all the battles that were fought in Leicestershire, the English Civil War was the most dramatic and terrible conflict. Many hundreds of people living in the county were uprooted and fled from their homes; in the case of Leicester, lost their lives. When the siege of Leicester was over, 700 people lay dead in the streets. In more recent conflicts memorials are erected throughout the county; where are the monuments to those killed at war in the later seventeenth century in Leicestershire? A few gravestones were put up, but most of the bodies were tipped into mass graves and forgotten. In the early nineteenth century a monument was constructed a few miles south of Market Harborough on the site of the fateful battle at Naseby. This photograph dates from the 1920s. The inscription reads:

To commemorate the great and decisive battle fought in this field on the XI day of June, MDCXLV, between the Royalist Army commanded by His Majesty King Charles First and the Parliament Forces headed by the Generals Fairfax and Cromwell, which terminated fatally for the Royal cause, led to the subversion of the throne, the altar, and the constitution, and for years flung the nation into the horrors of anarchy and civil war, learning a useful lesson to British Kings never to exceed the bounds of their just prerogative and to British subjects never to swerve from the allegiance due to their legitimate monarch. This pillar was erected by John and Mary Frances Fitzgerald, Lord and Lady of the Manor of Naseby, A.D. MDCCCXXIII.

Introduction

Why compile a book on battle sites in Leicestershire? Having written several books on the history of the county, it is impossible not to consider how one of the most famous of all English battles, the Battle of Bosworth Field, affects the recorded history of England. Apart from Bosworth, the sacking of Leicester during the English Civil War was another important occurrence. There were also a few individual skirmishes; that is all that affected the county on the whole. This is what many believe. But of course those observations could not be further from the truth. Leicestershire is the centre of England, the crossroads of history.

I first became interested in battles and skirmishes through discussions that took place between my parents before the Second World War. I think my father had a sense of guilt because he did not fight in the First World War; he worked in a protected occupation and failed the fitness test because of a badly damaged left leg. His younger brother joined up and was killed in the terrible battle at Arras in July 1917 and has no known grave. My mother witnessed a German army airship passing over the village of Wymondham in September 1916, and years later would comment on the engagement with the enemy at Paine sidings. When the Second World War began my father was registered at an open-cast mining site for iron ore, a reserved occupation. I can clearly remember standing on the lawn in front of our house with my mother and seeing waves of German bombers passing over the village in November 1940; much later we learned that these planes were bombing Coventry. My father worked on a night shift at the mining site to the east of Buckminster. My mother and I were watching German bombers passing over the village of Wymondham on 9 September 1940, during the usual German flights to Midland bombing sites, a regular experience in the winter months of 1940. On one unforgettable evening we both witnessed explosions and flashes of light in the direction of Buckminster less than two miles away as the crow flies. My mother shouted, 'That's on dad'. I did not understand my mother's comment. Next morning my father arrived back home on his motorbike, ashen-faced, with his clothing covered in clay and dust. His workforce had been bombed, he had dived under a goods wagon and this saved his life. Why bomb an open-cast mine? Was it a mistake? When it is extracted iron ore is stacked above the cut on the embankment, mixed with coal and coal slack and fired. It burns for about eight weeks, forming calcined ore. This burning ore glows in the night. Did the German bombers consider they were passing over a town that had been bombed previously, or did they know that this site was part of the war effort? Shortly after this my father was appointed as a ganger, helping to build Saltby airfield on Saltby Heath, under the direction of the War Office. When the airfield was virtually completed he witnessed one of the bombing raids on the runway by the German air force. For many years I kept the fins of an exploded incendiary bomb recovered from one of these two bombing raids that involved my father.

In 1952 at the age of eighteen I was called up for National Service into the Leicestershire Regiment, to be transferred to the military police. After training I spent the best part of eighteen months in Egypt, involved in the Suez Canal campaign. This sharpened my view on battles, especially skirmishes, and on the use of a revolver, rifle, Sten gun, tommy gun and the most reliable small-arms weapon, the Bren gun. I became a member of staff to the Commander-in-Chief of the Middle East Land Forces, as one of his group of personal bodyguards. The possibility of action against active terrorists was always at the front of my mind, especially as part of the squad patrolling the C-in-C's residence at night. Incoming submachine-gun fire 'is etched in your memory forever'!

On demobilisation I took up a career in education and my interest in war and battles became a hobby. With friends and family I attempted to visit all the sites in Leicestershire where a battle took place. In my opinion if two people attack or defend each other with an attempt to kill or maim and not for sport, this is a battle. For over fifty years I have collected information on what I consider battle sites in Leicestershire. During the English Civil War nearly every village and hamlet was involved. I doubt if this presentation is anywhere complete. Some terrible battles took place in the county and thousands of unrecorded graves exist. What records do survive are in the main written by the winners; this is not always the true story. In recent years much has been written about Bosworth Field and the correct position of the battle. Frankly, I consider the existing site, recorded by the Leicestershire County Council, is reasonably correct. Modern archivists translate medieval records. How many documents and the researchers and scribes who favoured Richard III would have survived, especially if Henry VIII, the victor's son, was aware of the observations and comments in favour of the victim that had surfaced during his lifetime?

Because of my interest in industrial archaeology, for many years I have endeavoured to describe what actually happened at the Battle of Saxby. As far as I know no one died as a result of this conflict. I believe it was a 'leftover campaign' of the medieval period orchestrated by a baronial relic, the 6th Lord Harborough.

This is my collection. Considerable individual research is still needed to add to this presentation, through controlled archaeological excavation of the numerous castle and battle sites, if funds become available. Then a multi-volume extension to this book could be published. In this compilation I have included comments, observations, my thoughts on the various battles and of course legends. I hope the reader will consider this a good story and that this book will help others to extend their knowledge, taking this as a guide for future research projects.

Trevor Hickman

1
Ratae to Leicester

Unquestionably Leicestershire was the cockpit of England, and many battles were fought over this shire county. Before the Romans arrived the local tribe, the Coritani, are thought to have occupied this area of land on the River Soar. The Roman occupation was not a sudden invasion with complete subjection of the populace. Julius Caesar invaded England in 55 BC, advanced around ten miles and retreated back to Gaul (France). A year later he attacked again with a stronger force, winning many battles, and crossed the River Thames, moving north. Roman occupation of the south of England had little or no effect on Leicester. It was under the Emperor Claudius 100 years later in AD 43 that the final conquest of England took place. Was the Celtic town on the River Soar that is now called Leicester defended? So much that could be part of the Bronze Age prior to the Roman occupation has been lost, but occasionally pre-Roman occupation evidence is uncovered in archaeological investigations.

The Romans built Ratae, a magnificent town which reached its peak by AD 350. Then the decline began, for the Roman legions were recalled to Rome. For 300 years the local populace had a life of peace. Few if any defensive positions existed to withstand the slow infiltration of the north German Anglo-Saxon invasion. Evidence exists that some Roman towns resisted the Saxon invasion, trying to protect their Romanised towns. Did this happen in Ratae? There is no conclusive evidence of battles and it is presumed the population of Ratae reduced so much that they literally faded away and the town became a desolate ruin.

Saxon pirates had attacked the coastal villages during the Roman occupation; with their flat-bottomed ships they moved up the many river systems off the North Sea. There are various theories as to how the Anglo-Saxons occupied Britain after the Roman invaders had left: the first is that bands of warriors moved across the countryside attacking occupied Romanised sites, killing and stealing as they progressed through the land. There is evidence that some isolated villas were attacked and sacked by the Saxons. In certain parts of the country defensive systems existed. The other theory is that as the Roman army gradually left England the warlike Saxons took their place. This was a very slow integration of the sparsely populated countryside. The Saxons were a farming community, not city dwellers, living in small farming communities of their own choosing. For 200 years after Roman legions left England what happened to Leicester is unknown. Possibly it was deserted. Rain, frost, floods and natural forces would have flattened Ratae. As the Saxons became more settled they occupied the area and erected wooden houses, principally wattle and daub, totally ignoring the Roman remains. This is obvious when archaeologists uncover Roman Leicester many metres below the present level of occupation.

In 586 Creoda was created the first King of Mercia, which encompassed all of the Midlands and much of eastern England. Possibly he could be considered the first King of England. This Saxon built churches, small towns and possibly began to build modern Leicester on the site of Ratae. This is very difficult to assess because gradually a Saxon law was evolved. Undoubtedly there would have been conflict between the paganism of the occupying Saxons and those who eventually embraced Christianity. A totally self-sufficient rural economy developed, to become the envy of other northern states of Europe. Anglo-Saxon England was ruled by church and state combined. This led to the formation of the English parishes, each with a priest and a place of worship.

From 757 to 796 Offa was King of Mercia, and Leicester expanded. By war, this king defeated the rival claimants to his throne, eventually controlling by conquest most of England south of the Humber. He issued the major form of royal coinage. He erected a defensive system, Offa's Dyke, to keep the warlike Welsh out of England. Saxon pirates had attacked the Romano-British, when the 'Sea Wolves', Vikings and Danes raided the islands of Britain. During the Roman occupation the local community throughout the country had become soft, allowing the Saxons to take over. Now after hundreds of years of reasonable peace, with a country devoted to a self-sufficient agricultural economy, the British were open to attack by adventurous invaders. So the Danelaw arrived.

This lithograph, drawn by John Flower and printed by W. Day of Queen Street, shows the Jewry Wall facing St Nicholas Church, *c.* 1820. The ruined walls of the Roman basilica date from the second century AD. Incorporated into the Roman walls is a medieval cottage. The town rose again from the Roman ruins, and it is not known whether it was ever completely deserted.

A Roman mosaic pavement has been re-sited at the Jewry Wall Museum in a display featuring a Roman house. Were such properties still occupied during the occupation of Ratae by the Saxon invaders?

It is possible that it all started after a raid with three longships with around 200 Viking pirates on the coast in Wessex. These men killed Offa's reeve, stole as much booty as they could and left before any opposition could be formed. At the end of the king's reign, in about 790, the attacks and pillage increased. The coasts of the British Isles were very easy pickings; the seaward-facing abbeys were a tremendous attraction and poorly defended, if at all. They contained splendid religious collections of gold, silver and precious stones. The Vikings, Norsemen and the Danes, through continuous raids, pillage and the taking of slaves, particularly females, developed a greater awareness of the soft belly of England and how it could be occupied by controlled invasion. Funding was easily obtained, with an axe splitting the skull of a monk and relieving his church of its valuables. To a pagan civilisation this was a splendid adventure.

The Danelaw was a slow process which came to control most of Saxon England. Brilliant soldiers, possibly Vikings, in their mail and with their long two-handled battleaxe, and their skill with the longbow, were feared throughout Europe. The Danes moved wherever they liked from the sea into estuaries and along the navigable rivers. Fighting, plundering and eventually occupying the countryside, from many thousands of raids, the Danes proceeded to occupy England as a permanent home. The Saxon farming peasant, called from his home, leaving his plough and oxen, and with a crude shield and handmade spear, was no challenge to the north European invaders, trained in war.

The occupation of England by the Danish invaders was an uncertain time. Saxon leaders were repeatedly defeated in war by the well-trained Danish armies. Leicester became part of Danish Mercia, either by conquest or by gradual infiltration by aggressive occupiers seeking to expand the Danish Empire. Resentment against the Danes would have been considerable, but the Saxon peasant could do little. Resentment of the Danelaw by the Saxons was considerable, and resistance was continual.

Egbert, King of Wessex 802–39, defeated Beornwulf of Mercia, and was considered to be the first monarch of all England. He was a Saxon king. During his lifetime he never completely controlled the Danes, who continued to infiltrate the countryside.

His son, Ethelwulf (839–58), continued the fight, training the farming community. He produced a son, Alfred (871–901), who took up arms against the Danes, but suffered much, because of poor-quality troops. He developed an excellent system of guerrilla warfare, repeatedly defeating the Danes, but never completely regaining the whole country. Small armies attacked the Danes throughout the shires, winning back some towns. Danelaw and paganism still ruled. Alfred trained his children and relatives in war. His daughter Ethelfleda, born in 869, goes down in history as Leicester's greatest princess. In 911 she married Ethelred, Earl of Mercia, part of Danish Mercia. In 918 her husband died. Through his continual illness she had controlled Mercia with difficulty, in opposition to the Danes. A devoted Christian, her mission to remove paganism from the land, she gathered together a reasonably trained army and in 917 she attacked Towcester and set up her government in place of Danelaw. Advancing on Leicester, a small market town with very little fortification, she overran the Danish fortifications leading from the front. Taking no prisoners, all the Danes were put to the sword. Possibly she was wounded in this battle, as sword cuts

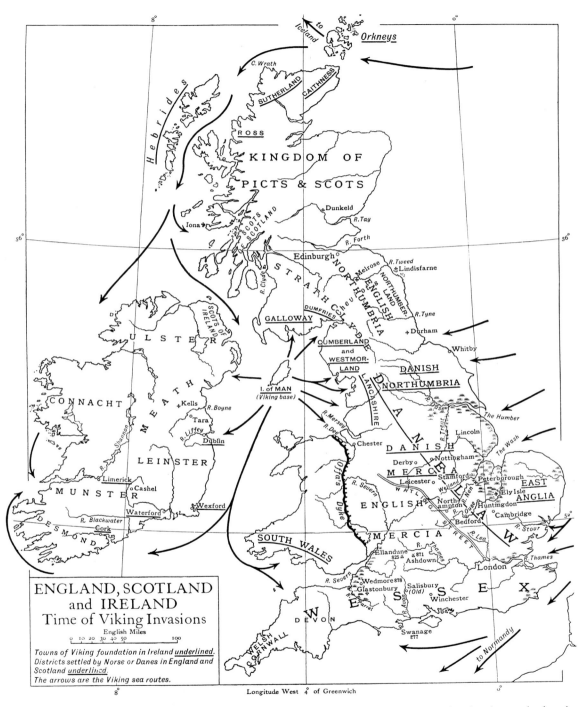

ENGLAND, SCOTLAND and IRELAND
Time of Viking Invasions
English Miles
0 10 20 30 40 50   100

Towns of Viking foundation in Ireland underlined.
Districts settled by Norse or Danes in England and Scotland underlined.
The arrows are the Viking sea routes.

Longitude West 4° of Greenwich

This is an attempt to place on record how Britain was affected during the continuous battles that took place in the ninth century, and the occupation of the islands. The map was engraved by Emery Walker in 1926.

could eventually prove to be fatal. On 12 June 918 she died in her bed at Tamworth, and was buried at Gloucester, so completing nearly fifty years as a devoted Christian on her death as the Lady of Mercia.

When the Memorial Clock Tower was erected in the centre of Leicester in December 1868, considerable discussion took place on who should stand in the niches on the tower. Simon de Montfort, William Wigston, Sir Thomas White and Gabriel Newton were chosen. Ethelfleda should have stood there rather than some of these less well-known contributors to the development of the town.

On the death of Alfred in 901, Edward the Elder, Alfred's son, took on the Danes; his father had chosen him to run Wessex and he can be considered king from 899 to 924. He defeated the main Danish claimants to the throne, and enjoyed considerable success in battle. He routed the Danes in a series of engagements, gaining control of Nottingham, Derby, Lincoln, Leicester and Stamford, fortifying these Midland towns. On the death of Edward the Elder, his son Athelstan became king (924–39). He was crowned in Kingston upon Thames and became the first Saxon king to effectively control all of England with the exception of Danish Cumbria. In 937 he won a very critical battle in Cumbria, destroying a Viking–Scottish coalition. For a short period of time he endeavoured to relieve the plight of the downtrodden Saxons, although the Danish problem still existed. On the death of Athelstan in 939 the Norse King Olaf II successfully, through various battles, gained control of much of the north of England. Edmund I was elected King of England in 939. Half-brother of Athelstan, he attacked Olaf and defeated him at Brunanburgh in 946, but was assassinated on 26 May 946 while at prayer at Canterbury. Edred, the youngest son of Edward the Elder, was crowned king in 946 when his brother was assassinated. Erik Bloodaxe in 948 attacked the north of England in Northumbria. Edred defeated the Danes in a series of battles in the north. In 954 he invaded Northumbria from the sea, this was a bloody invasion, killing Erik Bloodaxe. Edred appointed Oswulf as the earl of the northern counties, but died in his early twenties in 955. At the age of fifteen in 955, Edwy succeeded his uncle Edred as king, but proved a corrupt and incompetent ruler. Civil war among the Saxons was on the verge of a disaster as the Northumbrians and the Mercians denounced their king. Eventually Edwy was allowed to control part of the country south of the Thames.

The Saxon kingdom of England was in turmoil. Edgar was considered to be King of England from 957 to 975, with Edwy king in the south of the country. Edwy died in 959. Edgar attempted to unify the country. He made peace with most of the occupying Danes, converted them to Christianity, and built numerous monasteries. He was created 'Emperor of Britain' by the Archbishop of Canterbury at Bath in 973, although he did not rule all of Britain as there were two Scots kings, Malcolm and Kenneth, north of the border. King Alfred is credited with defeating the Danes. Of course he did not. These Scandinavian warriors brought their children and became integrated with the Saxons. Danes were a dominant race, and through marriage they became part of the Saxon community.

Edgar's son, Edward the Martyr, succeeded his father when he was twelve in 975. He was the son of Edgar's first wife Ethelfleda. His crowning was disputed by his half-brother, the son of Edgar's second wife. At the age of fifteen he was

Egbert, 'the first King of England'. He reigned from 802 to 839. Egbert fought Beornwulf of Mercia twice, the second time in 827 near Swindon. This time Egbert was again victorious, killing Beornwulf in the process. During the wars of that period no prisoners were ever taken.

assassinated by being stabbed in the back at the entrance to Corfe Castle in Dorset. Ethelred II (the Unready), the son of Edgar's second wife, Emma of Norway, was created king in 978. The Scandinavian marriage integrated the Danes with the Saxons. Ethelred tried to buy off the Danes, giving land and gold with repeated payments known as 'Danegeld'. He fooled the Danes and in a terrible battle in 1002 he massacred thousands of Danes. This was a mistake. Sweyn Forkbeard, King of Norway and Denmark, was furious, not least because his sister Gunnhilde had been killed by Ethelred's troops at a battle at Oxford. Sweyn formed a large Scandinavian army and invaded England along the east coast. He enjoyed many successes, devastating fifteen Midland counties including Leicestershire, but was unable to conquer London. Ethelred fled to Normandy in 1013. Sweyn Forkbeard then reigned as King of England but he fell from his horse in 1014 and died. Ethelred returned from northern France and resumed the crown of England. This was contested by Canute (King of England 1014–1035), Sweyn Forkbeard's son. Ethelred the Unready was killed in a skirmish with Canute's troops in London in 1016. He had reigned as king involving much of the north of England. He fought Edmund Ironside at the Battle of Ashington; this Saxon choice of king was assassinated after this battle. Canute became king of all England. This Danish king was noted for his barbarity and ruthlessness against the Saxons. He granted equal rights to the occupying Danes and the Saxons. In his will he left Norway to his eldest son, Denmark to his third son. England he left to his second son, Harold I (Harefoot), who reigned from 1035 to 1040; the Danes maintained him as King of England. On the death of Harefoot in 1040, Hardicanute, King of Denmark, was elected King of England by the Danes. A violent king, he murdered the Earl of Northumbria and sacked most of Mercia, burning Worcester to the ground. He reigned for two years and was a most unpopular king. Fortunately he collapsed at a wedding and died from a heart attack.

In 1042 Edward the Confessor was invited to return to England from Normandy, where he had lived in exile. He was the eldest son of Ethelred II (Ironside), who had attempted to remove Canute from the throne. During Canute's reign many Saxons had considered Ironside as the true King of England. Half-Danish and half-Saxon, Edward the Confessor ruled England from 1042 to 1066. With his Catholic background, and through his involvement in the church in Normandy, he introduced Norman clergy throughout the country. London was one of the wealthiest cities in northern Europe, viewed with envy by many Danish landowners. Godwin, Earl of Wessex, supported the Danish throne. In the year 1052 he raised a large army, attacked London and took the city by force. The Confessor appealed for Norman help to restore his authority. Godwin died shortly after this battle for London and his son Harold became Earl of Wessex. Through Norman help he maintained his control over the country and regained his hold on London. Edward the Confessor had promised the throne of England to a Norman, not to a Dane. There was little or no support for a Norman to rule England. On Edward the Confessor's death in 1066 Harold took the throne, claiming his succession had been granted to him by the dying king. But William, Duke of Normandy, stated that Edward had promised him the crown two years earlier. So the stage was set for the Norman Conquest. Edward the Confessor was a well-intentioned king, deeply religious, granting much power to the church

King Alfred, grandson of Egbert, who did much to stabilise the country. Despite some success against the occupying Danes, he never managed to control the whole of England.

The statue of Ethelfleda, the Lady of Mercia, by B.J. Fletcher. This is an imaginary portrait of the princess. The original bronze statue stood in Victoria Park, Leicester, and was unveiled as the Edith Gittins memorial drinking fountain in August 1922. It was stolen in 1978. Jack Newport of Cosby was commissioned to create a replica, which was unveiled on site in August 1980, to be stolen again, returned, and repeatedly vandalised. Finally in 1990 a decision was made to position this small bronze statue on its original pedestal in the entrance hall of the City Rooms.

throughout England. His legacy is the abbey at Westminster. He was canonised in 1161 by Pope Alexander III.

So Harold II became King of England, the second son of Godwin, Earl of Kent, and Gytha, sister of Canute's Danish brother-in-law, half-Saxon and half-Danish. There were two claimants to his throne: Tostig, Harold's brother, and the Duke of Normandy. Tostig landed along the northern coasts with a sizeable army. A large fleet sailed up the Humber and at Stamford Bridge in Yorkshire, battle commenced. Harold's army totally routed Tostig's army. The latter was killed and most of his troops were slaughtered, for the taking of prisoners very rarely happened during these warlike times. The Duke of Normandy landed with his army at Pevensey in Sussex. Harold was 250 miles away and had to force-march to attack this invading army who had time to prepare for the battle. Even after a nine-day march Harold was only narrowly beaten in the engagement at Senlac near Hastings. Harold was killed, along with his two brothers, and so ended 600 years of Anglo-Saxon and Danish rule of England. A new age began with the Norman Conquest.

William I, the Conqueror, born in 1027, was the illegitimate son of Robert, Duke of Normandy. His mother was an unmarried Falaise tanner. His great-great-grandfather was a Viking pirate, an 'excellent pedigree' to become King of England. William I was crowned on Christmas Day 1066 in the new Westminster Abbey. He had learned the art of war in northern France, having trained a most efficient army of knights who were exclusively loyal to him. He waged war against the barons of Maine, Anjou, Brittany and the feudal King of France, and defeated them all. He fought for the throne of England and with his superior army he was successful. He transferred every large estate in England to the generals who supported him at Hastings, making them tenants-in-chief; some became very large landowners. He made them directly responsible to the crown, thus restoring England to effective central control, through regulating taxation. In 1085 he instigated the general survey of the kingdom, using commissioners to hold inquiries in every shire county, ensuring that everything that was taxable was included; this was recorded on long parchment rolls to be copied into two large volumes known as Domesday Book.

After his coronation William proceeded to suppress the Saxons and in some instances the Danish occupiers who were the landowners in the shire counties. In Leicester it would seem the occupation was unopposed, principally because it had suffered much during the previous 200 years. William built a castle in the town in 1068. It was a motte and bailey construction, consisting of an earthen mound surrounded by a ditch with a wooden palisade on the top of the mound. A court was constructed below the mound, the bailey surrounded by its own ditch with a rampart and stockade consisting of sharpened and pointed tree trunks, and a strongly constructed fence. There were interior wooden walkways to provide a defensive system from which archers could aim their arrows at attacking troops.

William I granted Leicester to Hugh de Grantmesnil for his support in invading England. This faithful knight had backed him in his wars in northern France. Hugh died in Leicester Castle in 1098, and his body was conveyed back to Normandy for burial. In 1087 William the Conqueror had died while at war in northern France. Hugh de Grantmesnil was in conflict with the newly

Goldar Sculp.

King Canute, a Dane, ruled England from 1014 to 1035. He subjected the predominantly Saxon country to Danish domination, granting equality to the conquering Danes with the indigenous Saxons. Danish control of England developed. After Canute's death in 1035 civil war raged throughout the country for thirty years, and life was cheap.

crowned King of England, William II (Rufus). This William was subjected to continual uprisings against his rule in Normandy, and problems with the Welsh and the Scots.

William II attacked Hugh de Grantmesnil's castle in Leicester, partially damaging the bailey walls. Hugh was granted a pardon by the king. On his father's death in 1093 Ivor de Grantmesnil inherited Leicester and other estates in England, joining Robert of Belesme against King Henry I, who was crowned in 1100 on the death of his father William Rufus, killed in the New Forest while hunting deer. It is considered that this was hardly an accident.

Henry I was the youngest son of William the Conqueror. He married a Saxon girl in an attempt to unify Britain. There was still much opposition to Normans running the country and internal differences with the ruling barons. Robert de Belesme commenced a private war against the king in 1101, causing much destruction in a battle at Leicester. When the king's army won the day, Robert de Belesme joined a crusade to Jerusalem to seek peace with Henry. In his absence the king granted Robert de Beaumont, Count of Meulon, Leicester and its castle. Henry I died in 1135, possibly from a heart attack. He left no heir, as his only son had been drowned when his ship sank in the English Channel when it hit the Casquet rocks.

Stephen then became king, though his was a weak claim to the throne, through his mother being William I's daughter. There was much opposition to Stephen because many ruling barons had their own favourites. The country was rocked by inter-baronial wars. Local landowners needed to defend their estates and all their castles became centres of defence. Church towers were castellated, offering a limited form of defence for the peasants. Manor houses were defended with moats. Robert de Beaumont, 1st Earl of Leicester, rebuilt Leicester Castle in about 1107. The new one was built of stone possibly replacing the wooden palisades with a rectangular keep. This was essential to defend his interests against marauding barons with their armies. Robert le Bossu succeeded his father on his death in 1118 and consolidated the stone structure inside the castle, possibly building a stone hall. The age of anarchy came to an end when Stephen died in 1154. He was succeeded by Henry Plantagenet, Count of Anjou. Having no son he had adopted Henry as his son and heir, the grandson of William the Conqueror. Henry II was considered the richest prince in Europe, and was the first Plantagenet king. He began his reign by destroying many of the castles that were erected and rebuilt. He sought control of the shire courts. In 1168 Robert Blanchmains succeeded his father Le Bossu. He joined in the rebellion against Henry II. The king's army attacked and burnt down the town of Leicester confiscating all of Blanchmains's estates. The stone-built castle held out against the besieging king's army. Blanchmains was eventually taken prisoner, and the castles at Leicester, Mountsorrel and Groby surrendered. The king ordered the demolition of Leicester Castle in the years 1176–7. Eventually Robert Blanchmains secured a pardon from the king and the restoration of his lands and castles, except Mountsorrel. He was allowed to rebuild parts of Leicester Castle, which became his home until he died in 1204. With his death the Beaumont line of Earls of Leicester came to an end. His daughters Amicia and Margaret inherited the estates, which were divided. Amicia took over the ownership of the castle. Taking the title of Countess of Leicester, she married Simon de Montfort, and their famous son and heir was Simon. Considerable problems occurred with the division of the town of Leicester, through various deaths and further alterations in wills to the inheritance of the extensive estate. Simon de Montfort secured his father's estate, including the castle at Leicester, by 1231.

Goldar Sculp.

William the Conqueror. After his victory over Harold II in 1066 he started to change the method of rule that had developed under Anglo-Saxon law and Danish barbarity. His generals were granted large parts of England. Where the ruling Saxons or Danes resisted they were killed. If they accepted the new systems and the Norman Conqueror's laws, they were integrated into the new system of controls. Castles were erected by his generals throughout the country, some of which were attacked by the local inhabitants. The Midlands were heavily defended with the building of many motte and bailey castles, originally to repel the local inhabitants but within a very short time to be used as defensive positions against groups of envious Norman barons.

In 1191 Henry II had died, and his rebellious sons had attempted to gain control of his throne, organising an uprising supported by various barons. His eldest son died before him and Richard I, Coeur de Lion, was crowned king. Richard, a 32-year-old warrior, spent most of his time on the Third Crusade to recover the Christian kingdom of Jerusalem. On his return from the crusade he was taken prisoner and held by the Austrian Emperor Henry VI for seventeen months. During Richard's absence his brother John headed an insurrection. This was suppressed by Richard when he returned to England. He only spent approximately six months of his reign in England, and was killed while fighting in Normandy against Philip II of France in 1199.

John, the youngest son of Henry II, was a quarrelsome king, and spent most of his reign fighting against his barons and certainly had disagreements with the Pope in Rome. John laid siege to many of the established castles and built others throughout the country, including Sauvey Castle to the east of Leicester. During John's reign Leicester Castle would appear to have been administrated by royal keepers on behalf of the king. Meanwhile, Simon de Montfort spent most of the early years of his life in Gascony in northern France. King John, on one of his tax-collecting furores with a small army throughout the shire counties, took ill in Nottinghamshire and died in Newark Castle in 1216. He was succeeded by his nine-year-old son, Henry III. During his minority the young king with a group of barons nominated William Marshall, Earl of Pembroke, as regent. The Earl of Pembroke was granted complete control of the Midlands. The local barons objected, raising their own taxes. Anarchy ruled once again throughout England. In 1264 Simon de Montfort took possession of Leicester Castle from the king's royal keeper. To endeavour to unify the country Simon entertained King Henry III and his son, Prince Edward, at Leicester Castle. At this time the living quarters must have been quite splendid. The outcome of this meeting was not successful, and within a few months a group of barons had elected Simon de Montfort as their leader and were at war with their king. Simon's army of barons defeated the king's army at Lewes and captured the king. Simon de Montfort, Earl of Leicester, formed the first parliament, and required that the king should accept a set of legally binding resolutions, known as the 'Mise of Lewes'. For approximately one year the Earl of Leicester's parliament attempted to enforce the law. The group of barons could not agree; one faction supported Leicester, the other the king. The opposing sides met in battle at Evesham, where without the help of his son Edward the king would have lost. Simon de Montfort was killed and his family forfeited their Leicestershire estates. After the Battle of Evesham, Edward, the king's son, effectively ruled England until his father's death in 1272. Henry III had granted his younger son, Edmund (Crouchback) the Earldom of Leicester in 1265; along with this were many castles and estates spread across the Midlands.

When Henry died Edward was on a Crusade in the Holy Land. An excellent soldier, he was crowned at Westminster Abbey in 1274. Earl Edmund died in 1296 and his son Thomas of Lancaster inherited the castle and the extensive estates in and around Leicester. Edward I rationalised the laws of the land, and defeated the Welsh, unifying their country with England, but never succeeded in completely defeating the Scots. Marching north to attack Robert Bruce he died in camp at a village near Carlisle. His only son, Edward II, succeeded in

Hugh de Grantmesnil, possibly under the direction of William I, built the first castle in Leicester in 1068, a motte and bailey construction consisting of a mound, moat and wooden palisade. This sketch was produced in the early part of the twentieth century from a stained-glass window in the church of the Abbey of St Evroult, in northern France. Hugh de Grantmesnil died on 22 February 1098, fairly certainly in his castle at Leicester, aged about seventy-eight. On his death his body was preserved in salt and conveyed to Normandy to be interred in the Abbey of St Evroult.

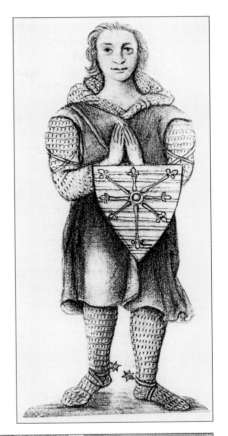

This drawing was produced by Robert Throsby and engraved by J. Swaine in 1795. It shows the River Soar with the remains of Hugh de Grantmesnil's castle of 1068. The mound is in the centre, to the left is St Mary's Church; part of the remains of Leicester Castle, built in 1108, can also be seen.

1307. He was a very weak king. As he had no experience of war he could not control his barons and anarchy returned to the British Isles. Thomas of Lancaster raised a small army against the king in Leicester. He was not successful because he had not gained sufficient support from local barons. Under the orders of the king he was executed in 1322. The keepership of the estates and the castles was entrusted to Roger de Beler, who held this commission for one year. He had been a good friend of Thomas of Lancaster, and must have supported the king at the time of Thomas's execution. The king confirmed him as a knight of the realm living at the Manor House at Kirby (Bellars). He held the Framland Hundred as magistrate and was one of the Barons of the Exchequer granted by the king in 1322. During the conflict with the king, Thomas of Lancaster was joined by Roger la Zouch of Lubbesthorpe and Ralph la Zouch of Ashby de la Zouch; these two barons with others attacked the home of Hugh le Despencer at the manor house of Loughborough with their small army, sacking the house. The king was furious and instructed Sir Roger de Beler to arrest and appoint a special commission to try the offenders on 28 May 1322. Under a weak king no satisfactory conclusion was arrived at. The result was that Sir Roger la Zouch, Robert de Helewell and Sir Eustace de Folville formed a small army to attack and kill Sir Roger de Beler, who they considered was a traitor to their cause by supporting the king against Thomas of Lancaster. While moving around the country de Beler, as the king's commissioner, was protected by a small mobile army. These two small armies met in the valley near Rearsby when Sir Roger was travelling to Leicester to act as the presiding judge in the city courts (see p. 159). Sir Roger de Beler was killed; Sir Eustace de Folville died through being struck down with an arrow three days later.

The year 1326 was a terrible one for Edward II; he had lost the Battle of Bannockburn in Scotland. An influential baron, Roger Mortimer, Earl of March, who had been banished to France, invaded England, with Isabella, the estranged wife of the king. A number of small battles and skirmishes took place at Glamorgan, where the king was captured and imprisoned by Mortimer and Isabella on 16 November 1326. In January 1327 a parliament was held in Westminster, and under the direction of Mortimer the king's son was chosen to be king as Edward III. Edward II was murdered in Berkeley Castle on 21 September 1328.

At the age of fifteen Edward III became king under the sinister baron, Mortimer, who technically held the power of the throne. On 28 February 1327 Edward III visited Leicester Castle with Mortimer to arrange the court of inquiry on the murder of Sir Roger de Beler, under the hospitality of the Earl of Leicester, Henry de Lancaster. Sir John Hamelin of Wymondham was appointed commissioner to hunt down the gang of barons who had killed Sir Roger de Belers. Three years later a local baronial war took place in Leicestershire. The Earl of Leicester objected to the way Mortimer and Isabella controlled the country. Roger Mortimer, Earl of March, John of Eltham, Earl of Cornwall, and Edmund Boteler, Earl of Ormond, formed a large army and attacked Leicester and the surrounding towns and villages while the Earl of Leicester was absent. They sacked Leicester Castle, and many churches and notable houses, stealing gold and silver ornaments and agricultural produce, and carrying it away on stolen carts. Many barons turned against Mortimer. In October 1330 Roger Mortimer was staying at Nottingham Castle. By this time the king, aged nearly

William (II) Rufus. His father, the Conqueror, never completely brought the whole of England under his control and at his death rebellious barons and submissive Saxons caused trouble against Rufus. Hugh de Grantmesnil was one of the rebellious barons who objected to King William's laws. The king attacked Leicester Castle with a small army, and breached the bailey walls, but the castle withstood the ensuing siege. The king retreated, as there were more pressing needs against the Welsh. He ruled badly for thirteen years and may have been assassinated in the New Forest.

Henry I, the youngest son of William I. Robert de Belesme controlled most of Leicestershire with Ivor de Grantemesnil. Belesme was one of the ruling barons who objected to Henry being made king, and started a private war against Henry in 1101. At the Battle of Leicester the king's army won, resulting in the town of Leicester being sacked. Robert de Belesme fled the field and joined a crusade to Jerusalem as a penance.

eighteen, was endeavouring to throw off his degrading dependence on Mortimer, and with some loyal barons he entered Nottingham Castle via a subterranean passage, from the series of caves near the famous Trip to Jerusalem inn. This passageway into the castle is still maintained and is open to the public on certain days. Having captured Mortimer, the king supervised his trial and Mortimer was found guilty of treason and hanged at Tyburn on 29 November. Isabella, the king's mother, went into quiet retirement. Edward III visited Leicester Castle in 1323 on his way north to make war in Scotland. He defeated the Scots at Halidon Hill on 19 July 1333, but wars with the Scots continued. On numerous occasions Philippa, Edward's queen, visited Leicester and stayed overnight in the castle. In August 1348 the Black Death reached England; one-third of the total population died over the next twelve months. Edward III's armies were decimated and he lost all of his conquests. In 1377 the king died, having suffered from senile dementia for the last few years of his life. In 1361 John of Gaunt, Duke of Lancaster, became Earl of Leicester through marriage to Blanche, one of the daughters of Henry, Duke of Lancaster, who had held Leicester under the direction of the king. John of Gaunt spent considerable money on improving the standing of Leicester Castle. The time of John of Gaunt was the most splendid period of the castle's activities. When visiting the site of the motte and bailey it is possible to see the vandalised entrance of John of Gaunt's cellar on the left of the steps, which was wantonly destroyed.

The king's grandson Richard II succeeded at the age of nine. Richard was the son of the Black Prince, the king's eldest son, who had died in 1376. The young king's uncle, John of Gaunt, held considerable power throughout the country and particularly in Leicestershire. On 1 August 1390 the Earl of Leicester entertained the king and queen with many noble guests at the splendid castle at Leicester.

> Lo on the mound in days of feudal pride
> Thy tow'ring Castle frown'd above the tide;
> Flung wide her gates, where troops of vassals met
> With awe the brow of high Plantagenet.

For the last two years of his life, John of Gaunt lived in his castle, and died there on 3 February 1399. On his uncle's death Richard confiscated all John of Gaunt's lands, including Leicestershire. In his will he had passed all of these lands on to his son, Henry Bolingbroke. The barons waged war on the king once again, and Richard lost the ensuing battle at Chester near Flint Castle, on 19 August 1399. He was conveyed to London and on this journey he was imprisoned in Leicester Castle for a few days, before being judged by the barons at the Tower of London. Bolingbroke was elected king. Richard II was imprisoned in Pontefract Castle; shortly after his internment, the young king died.

When Bolingbroke succeeded to the throne of England as Henry IV in 1399 this Lancastrian king decreed that Leicester Castle cease to be a ducal residence, and its importance gradually declined. Henry IV visited Leicester on a number of occasions on state duties, staying for a few days in Leicester Castle in November 1410. He died on 20 March 1413. Harry of Monmouth came to the throne as Henry V. His connection with Leicester Castle is that he erected a tomb over the remains of his mother in the castle's chapel. This young king is remembered for winning the famous Battle of Agincourt with his English

Leicester Castle. This is an early eighteenth-century engraving from a drawing or painting of the castle. It may be a copy of an early sixteenth-century illustration that has been lost. Evidence of the deterioration of the building is clearly shown.

Stephen, crowned in 1135. This was the 'age of anarchy', and for nineteen years this king ruled badly. The baronial wars ravaged the countryside.

archers. He was a shrewd military tactician, and the barons supported him on his numerous military adventures. He died at the age of thirty-five, worn out through the continuous hardships of his many campaigns, and his ten-month-old son succeeded him as Henry VI.

During this king's minority the kingdoms were controlled by Richard Beauchamp, Earl of Warwick, and his uncles John, Duke of Bedford, and Humphrey, Duke of Gloucester. This child king was displayed to all and sundry. The Duke of Bedford knighted the youngster at Leicester Castle in May 1426. Henry assumed personal control at the age of fifteen. During the years 1461–70 the king suffered from bouts of mental illness. Margaret of Anjou, the queen, appointed a protector, Richard, Duke of York. The Lancastrian group opposed this, and the first battle of the thirty years of civil war to be known as the Wars of the Roses took place at St Albans on 22 May 1455. The Lancastrians lost. Numerous battles were fought throughout England, many barons were killed, and the king was held in the Tower of London. For one year he was accepted as king by some of the baronial nobles, only to be murdered in the Tower of London in 1471.

Edward IV, the son of Richard Plantagenet, Duke of York, became King of England and Wales in 1461. He was considered by many barons as the legitimate heir to the throne, through force of arms and vast sums of money available through taxation and extreme wealth from the coffers of Edward, Duke of York. After a few short battles Edward established a reasonably stable country for twelve years. He visited Leicester on numerous occasions; possibly the most important was in 1471, when he raised an army in Lincolnshire and Leicestershire, staying at the castle on his way south to Barnet on 14 April 1471. At Barnet he defeated the Earl of Warwick and his Lancastrian supporters, and won a further battle on 4 May 1471. The inhabitants of Leicester were firm supporters of the Yorkists in this terrible civil war. It is amazing that any culture or expansion of the economy ever survived. Edward certainly did not alienate the citizens of London. He died at Westminster on 9 April 1483.

Edward V, a boy of twelve, inherited the crown. His father's brother Richard, Duke of Gloucester, was confirmed as Protector, Defender of the Realm and guardian of the young king's person. The young king's uncle demanded of the queen, Elizabeth Woodville, that he should also protect the king's brother Richard. Both of these two youngsters, his nephews, were placed in the Tower of London under his protection. He then declared Edward V and his younger brother illegitimate, which meant they could not inherit the crown of England. These two youngsters were murdered in the Tower of London. Lord Hastings, whose residence was at Ashby de la Zouch Castle, supported the young king, Edward V. He was arrested and beheaded, without a trial.

If Richard III killed these two royal children it was a shocking crime, even in the tumultuous times of the fifteenth century. Nobles and royalty killed each other continually in the many minor wars and battles that occurred in England, but the disappearance of these two royal children was something that many of the ruthless nobles from supporters of both Yorkist and Lancastrian sides could not stomach. For nearly two years Richard ruled England with a rod of iron, and executed most of his enemies. In 1482 his only son died and the following year his queen. He was crowned on 26 June 1483. On 18 August 1483 he stayed in Leicester Castle on his

This is an engraving from a painting produced by
C.R. Leslie RA in the early part of the nineteenth
century. It is a typical Victorian romantic impression of
how the drunken revellers celebrated a victory during
the baronial wars. A child is astride a broken lance.
The armoured knight looks on slightly amused in the
castle hall.

The remains of Leicester Castle, drawn by John Throsby
and engraved by J. Walker in 1791. Compare it with the
engraving published four years later and seen on p. 21.
In this illustration the river is overgrown with greenery
and the castle buildings show considerable changes. It is
difficult to assess which drawing supersedes the other.
The publication date is not necessarily the date when the
original drawing was produced.

tour across the Midland counties, then on to Nottingham and York. On 21 October 1483 he returned to Leicester Castle, and remained there until 26 October 1483. The countryside was in rebellion and many minor skirmishes took place. Richard had a fine well-trained small army, so defeated many of the rebellious nobles. Even the Yorkist fellow-conspirators were against him. A group of noblemen, Lancastrian and Yorkist, invited Henry Tudor, Earl of Richmond, who had been banished to Brittany by the crown, to assume the throne of England.

The Wars of the Roses was reaching its peak. An army was formed under Henry Tudor, and Richard III increased the size of his well-trained force. In August 1485 the king was staying at Nottingham Castle. He divided his army into divisions and marched to Leicester on Sunday 20 August 1485. He stayed at the Blue Boar Inn. Why he did not use the royal quarters at Leicester Castle is not known. Possibly Richard III favoured Nottingham Castle, his East Midlands headquarters, and commenced to demolish Leicester Castle and its walls. On 21 August 1485 Richard III marched to Bosworth Field over Bow Bridge across the River Soar to his place in history. The next day he was killed in the battle through the defection of the Stanley family.

Henry Tudor, Earl of Richmond, was crowned King of England on the battlefield. The Wars of the Roses were virtually over. Henry VII married Edward IV's Yorkist daughter, thus uniting the warring factions in the House of Tudor. Henry marched through Leicester on his way to the battle at Stoke Field that took place on 16 June 1487. The battlefield lies south-west of Newark-on-Trent off the Fosse Way/A46 near the village of Fiskerton, on the banks of the River Trent. With the end of the civil war in England after the battle at Stoke Field, a form of stability existed throughout the country. Certainly no major conflict took place in Leicestershire until the middle of the seventeenth century.

Charles I was born in Scotland in 1600, the son of James VI of Scotland and I of England. A staunch Protestant, his mother was Danish and he married Henrietta Maria, daughter of King Henry I of France, a loyal Roman Catholic. Charles expected to run Britain by divine right and did not call a parliament at Westminster for eleven years. Some of the descendants of the medieval barons and 'the man in the street' protested against this king, who was a thoroughly bad politician. Opinions divided as Charles attempted to gain backing from the country at large. He attracted some support from his friends and wealthy landowners, especially in Leicestershire. He visited Leicester on at least two occasions, which cost the town considerable money. On his last visit, in 1638, he expected the corporation to raise funds for munitions for the king's service.

A parliament had been formed in London in defiance of the king. The town of Leicester was on the Parliamentary side, but many wealthy local families supported the king, some the Parliament, and others sat on the fence. Archdale Palmer of Wanlip was High Sheriff of Leicestershire and backed the Parliamentary movement. The Earl of Stamford, with Wanlip's backing, entered Leicester and emptied the town's magazine of arms and ammunition, conveying this to his house at Bradgate. On 11 June 1642 Charles I issued his first commission of array to the High Sheriff to support Charles and train a group of the citizens of Leicestershire on his behalf. By writ of 25 June 1642 the king removed Archdale Palmer from office and appointed Henry Hastings, son of the Earl of Huntingdon, with a royal commission. Hastings arrived at Leicester with a small army of about 100 troops

Simon de Montfort, a statue that stands on the Clock Tower Memorial in the centre of Leicester. De Montfort married Henry III's sister in 1235. In 1264 he led an army of barons against his king, defeating him at Lewes. He and fifteen barons ruled England for nearly twelve months, only to be beaten at the Battle of Evesham with an army led by the future King of England, Edward I.

The interior of the courthouse referred to as Leicester Castle in 1866, in a drawing by H. Goddard, engraved by J.H. Keux.

and confronted Palmer who had gathered together a well-armed group of supporters at Horse Fair Leas off The Newarke. Hastings proclaimed the King's Writ. Battle commenced, but a heavy shower of rain dampened the powder and the antagonists, a few troops were injured from drawn swords, and no lives were lost. This was the forerunner of the terrible civil war that was to follow.

On 22 July 1642 Charles again visited Leicester on his journey around England to gather support against the Parliamentary faction. Many towns 'locked their gates' against the king. His reception in Leicester aggravated the division that now existed between the citizens and the ruling class who controlled parts of Leicestershire. He returned to Leicester on 24 August 1642, and stayed at Cavendish House, Leicester Abbey. The following day he journeyed on and raised the Royal Standard at Nottingham Castle, and the civil war officially began. Two days later, on 26 August, Prince Rupert attacked Bradgate House with the Royalist cavalry to retrieve the munitions that the Earl of Stamford had removed from Leicester. The occupants had fled. He demanded a fine of £2,000 from the citizens of Leicester. During winter 1642/3 the setting up of the Parliamentary association of eight Midlands counties was completed. Skirmishes, small battles and major conflicts between the two opposing forces took place throughout Leicestershire.

The major problem in the Midlands according to the king was Leicester, a Parliamentary town. On 27 May 1645 2,000 Royalist cavalry started encircling the town. Parliamentary cavalry under the direction of Major Babington and Major Inness skirmished with Sir Marmaduke Landale's Royalist cavalry. Frantic defence systems were built to protect the town, using existing features along with temporary barricades. Leicester was very poorly defended. The governor, Sir Robert Pye, controlled a garrison of just over 2,000 men, the majority of whom were mercenaries from Scotland, who hated King Charles. On 29 May the main body of the Royalist army arrived with Rupert and Charles directing the siege, at the head of possibly as many as 10,000 troops. Prince Rupert's battery was sited on the Rawdykes. On p. 48 a suggested plan of the siege is published from records made available in the nineteenth century. Approximately half of the king's army were foot soldiers. The cavalry consisted of:

King's and Queen's Troop	130
Prince Rupert's Regiment	540
Prince Maurice	120
Lord Loughborough	100
Colonel Catyes	200
Earl of Northampton	850
Colonel Howard	880
Sir Marmaduke Langdale and Sir William Blackstone	1,500
Sir Richard Willys	1,200
Total Regiments of Horse	5,520

Attacking positions were laid out around the town. It was decided that the main assault would be made against The Newarke. At noon on 30 May 1645 Prince Rupert fired a ranging shot from his cannon in that direction. Then he offered a

The remains of part of the castle built after 1108 that have been incorporated into the south-facing wall of Leicester Castle Courthouse. This photograph is from August 2003.

Students from De Montfort University standing on top of the castle mound, Leicester Castle, August 2003.

This view from the top of the castle mound features part of the Turret Gateway to the castle, August 2003. The gateway is referred to by many local historians as Rupert's gateway.

pardon to the town if the garrison would surrender. The governor held a meeting in the Guildhall but those present could not agree to Prince Rupert's terms. Rupert lost patience; at 2.30 p.m. he commenced the bombardment and the walls and barricades in front of The Newarke were breached. At midnight the king ordered a general attack on the town with the regiment of foot soldiers, Sir B. Astley's division from Leicester Abbey and Sir H. Baird's foot soldiers along Belgrave Gate. Prince Rupert's infantry along with Colonel Leslie's division simultaneously attacked The Newarke and the barricades at Horse Fair Leas. Throughout the town the perimeter defences collapsed. A stand was made in the market square, where a ferocious engagement was made between the King's and Queen's Troop and the remnants of the town's cavalry, who were virtually killed to a man. The defenders fought fiercely at The Newarke and succeeded in repulsing Colonel Leslie's foot soldiers. The king ordered his own Footguards to join in the assault on the collapsed defences.

Eventually a last stand was made in the fortifications in The Newarke. Heavy fighting had taken place throughout the town, and civilians were involved in attacking passing Royalist troops from barricaded houses, especially from overlooking upper-room windows. Approximately 600 troops fought to the last in The Newarke magazine. Some were allowed to surrender: civilians, men and women who had fought against the Royalists; the Scottish soldiers were slaughtered as they were captured. Skirmishing continued throughout the night. Ten mounted Parliamentary cavalry escaped by crossing the River Soar at Black Friars. Over 500 defenders were killed, and many died later from their wounds. Approximately 200 Royalists were killed.

The king rested at Leicester Abbey overnight. He passed through the town on his horse after the battle, commenting that the rebels should expect no quarter. Henry Hastings was made the Royalist governor of the town with a garrison of 1,200 men. This Royalist success was short-lived, however, as the famous Battle of Naseby took place a fortnight later just over the county border near Market Harborough. The Royalist army suffered a total defeat on 14 June 1645. After a token siege on 18 June, Hastings surrendered Leicester to General Fairfax, who appointed General John Needham as governor. The English Civil War brought to an end major conflicts in Leicester and the surrounding district.

No further major battles ever took place in Leicestershire. It was not until the First World War that any military conflicts could be considered as battles. Military airships flew over the county dropping bombs, notably on Loughborough on 31 January 1916. There was no retaliation. A skirmish involving a 'Zeppelin' also occurred near Wymondham on 2 September 1916.

Just over twenty years after the Armistice that marked the end of the First World War, the Second World War broke out. Airfields received direct hits as a result of bombing raids, and troops and RAF personnel retaliated. The cities and towns were a different problem: if an anti-aircraft gun is fired at an attacking plane, the shells will explode and the shrapnel returns to earth. Equally, fire a machine-gun at an attacking plane and the arc of fire must be controlled. Thousands of people have been killed and wounded by friendly fire from descending shrapnel and bullets. This is why little or no defence of built-up areas in Leicestershire took place. Two recorded positions are at Stoughton and Barkby, at both of which return fire took place, and of course the many local airfields.

A plan of Leicester Castle, drawn and published in 1906.

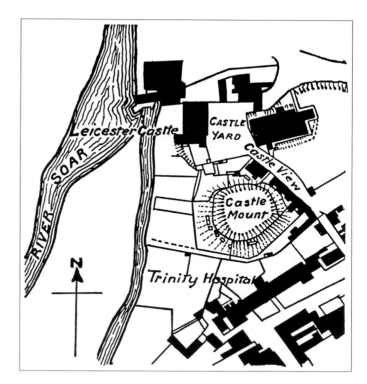

The remains of one of the walls in the gardens, Leicester Castle, August 2003.

Edward I, the 'Hammer of the Scots'; King of England, Wales, Scotland and Ireland 1272–1307. He defeated and killed Simon de Montfort and subdued the barons who opposed the king.

Edward II (1307 to 1327) was a weak king, and the barons took advantage of his mild disposition. One of the dissenting barons, Roger Mortimer, gained power and murdered him at Berkeley Castle.

Edward III succeeded to the throne at the age of four, reigned from 1327 to 1377, and took revenge on Mortimer for the death of his father.

John of Gaunt, Earl of Leicester, was the father of King Henry IV.

Leicester's coat of arms in 1904, a wyvern surrounding a red shield displaying a cinqefoil. The wyvern was incorporated into the arms of Henry, Earl of Leicester, in 1361. Cinqefoils were part of the seal of the town of Leicester as early as 1334. Coats of arms were painted on the shield carried by the leader of any armed force, especially in the baronial wars. The groups could identify each other and form up with their leader. When the fight became spread across the battlefield, shields, flags and pennants – the colours – became the visual rallying point. Military flags and emblems still feature in military campaigns today.

LEICESTER.

A nineteenth-century wood engraving of the Tudor gateway leading into the castle yard from Castle Street, c. 1840.

Harry Bolingbroke, son of John of Gaunt. Bolingbroke defeated Richard II in battle in 1399, became king and took the title of Henry IV. This a typical early Victorian drawing.

Henry IV, in this engraving, is seen receiving the crown from Richard II in 1399. He later downgraded Leicester Castle.

Henry VI succeeded to the throne before his first birthday. He inherited his kingdom from his famous father, Henry V, the victor over the French at Agincourt in 1415.

Edward IV, son of Richard Plantagenet, Duke of York. During his reign, the Yorkist faction controlled England and were the victors in many minor battles. In 1471 from his base at Leicester Castle he raised an army from the population of Leicestershire and Lincolnshire, so winning the battle at Barnet in April, when he defeated the Lancastrian army of the Earl of Warwick.

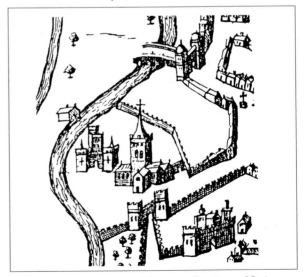

King Henry VII, victor at the Battle of Bosworth in 1485.

A detail from John Speede's 1610 drawing of Leicester. It features the castle with St Mary's Church near the River Soar.

Richard III, who visited and resided at Leicester Castle on numerous occasions. In 1980 the Richard III Society erected this monument to the king in the Leicester Castle grounds. In the background the remains of the castle are visible and St Mary's Church stands high above the trees. Continually vandalised, this statue has been moved to a more prominent position and now stands outside the west entrance to the castle gardens.

Bow Bridge and King Richard's Bridge in an engraving published in the eighteenth century from an inaccurate composite drawing. In the foreground stand fifteenth-century soldiers. Behind Bow Bridge are the ruins of Grey Friars monastery where the remains of the king were buried. The engraving of the collegiate church is included in the background where the king's lying in state took place.

This is a more accurate engraving of King Richard's Bridge, published in 1791. Legend has it that the king's army left Leicester over this bridge for the Battle of Bosworth in 1485. When the two engravings reproduced on this page were originally published there was still considerable support for the Plantagenet king, Richard III. Henry VIII was certainly not a more suitable king than Richard. He murdered his wives; there is no conclusive proof that Richard murdered his nephews. It must be remembered that the Tudors compiled the information concerning the death of Richard's nephews.

This drawing of King Richard's Bridge was produced in the late nineteenth century by G. Spawton Carlow and published in 1881. On the house overlooking the River Soar is a memorial erected to record the site where Richard's remains were thrown into the river. When this building was demolished the memorial was saved and was positioned near the existing King Richard's Bridge.

Right: The memorial that has been positioned near King Richard's Bridge on King Richard's Road.

The Old Blue Boar from a drawing published in 1826 by John Flower. It was in this inn that Richard III stayed before his final battle at Bosworth Field in 1485. A developer demolished this famous building in 1836.

King Richard's Bridge, August 2003. At either end of the parapet has been positioned a plaque, photographs of which appear here. To the right, behind the shrubbery, stands the monument opposite (left).

The two plaques were erected on King Richard's Bridge in 1862. Legend has it that a local wise woman witnessed King Richard's spur striking a projecting part of the bridge. She was asked to predict the outcome of the battle. She said that where his spur struck this bridge, his head should be broken.

THIS BRIDGE WAS ERECTED BY THE CORPORATION OF LEICESTER IN THE MAYORALTY OF SAMUEL VICCARS ESQ: A.D.1862. ON THE SITE OF THE ANCIENT BOW BRIDGE OVER WHICH KING RICHARD III PASSED AT THE HEAD OF HIS ARMY TO THE BATTLE OF BOSWORTH FIELD. AUGUST 22nd 1485. JOSEPH WHETSTONE CHAIRMAN OF THE HIGHWAY COMMITTEE SAMUEL STONE TOWN CLERK E.L. STEPHENS BOROUGH SURVEYOR

"UPON THIS BRIDGE [AS TRADITION HATH DELIVERED] STOOD A STONE OF SOME HEIGHT, AGAINST WHICH KING RICHARD, AS HE PASSED TOWARD BOSWORTH, BY CHANCE STRUCK HIS SPUR; AND AGAINST THE SAME STONE, AS HE WAS BROUGHT BACK HANGING BY THE HORSE SIDE, HIS HEAD WAS DASHED AND BROKEN; AS A WISEWOMAN [FORSOOTH] HAD FORETOLD, WHO BEFORE RICHARD'S GOING TO BATTLE, BEING ASKED OF HIS SUCCESS, SAID THAT WHERE HIS SPUR STRUCK, HIS HEAD SHOULD BE BROKEN." SPEED'S HISTORY OF GREAT BRITAIN

Charles I reigned from 1625 to 1649. He lived in the past; possibly he considered he should reign as a medieval king and certainly in 1642 he expected to control the country by force of arms. A poor politician, he failed to understand the feelings of the people in many respects during the early years of the Civil War. This was a repeat of the baronial wars. Oliver Cromwell changed that. He was a Huntingdonshire landowner and influenced the common man to fight against what many people considered was a corrupt king. Religion became part of Cromwell's mission, which could be construed as a form of socialism, and led to the formation of a republic.

In 1777 John Prior of Ashby de la Zouch completed his map of Leicestershire and in 1779 it was published in London. After the sacking of Leicester by Charles I's army it took years to rebuild the town. In this section from Prior's map the town and district of Leicester clearly indicates the Leicester battlefield of 1645. The town had hardly expanded into the surrounding countryside.

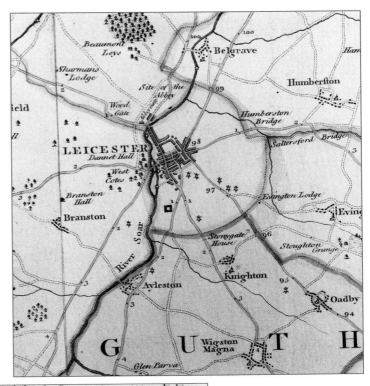

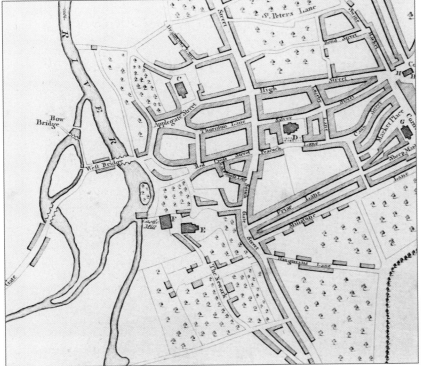

John Prior's plan of Leicester in 1777. In this extract, bridges crossing the River Soar are clearly indicated. Bow Bridge and King Richard's Bridge still cross the river, and the watermill, a large construction, is near the castle. The letters printed on this plan are: C. St Nicholas, D. St Martins, E. St Mary's, F. The Castle, G. The Exchange, H. Assembly Room.

Prince Rupert (1619–82), Count Palatine of the Rhine and Duke of Bavaria, nephew of Charles I, son of Elizabeth, daughter of James I, King Charles's father. Rupert attended St John's College, Oxford, but did not take kindly to education and his uncle's control, so joined his family in the Netherlands. He developed into a fine soldier, gaining experience in the many minor wars in Europe. In July 1642 Charles recalled him to England. He became general of horse, answerable only to the king. In November 1644 he was appointed general of the whole Royalist army. The king's councillors resented the prince's independent role and did not support him with the necessary finances and persuaded the king to sack him. On the restoration of the monarchy Charles II invited the prince to return. Prince Rupert, Duke of Cornwall, was appointed as an admiral, and played a brilliant part in the Dutch wars. Many historians of the seventeenth century consider that if Prince Rupert had been granted complete support by the king and his financial supporters there would have been a different outcome to the English Civil War.

Prince Rupert on the Raw Dykes preparing to attack Leicester with cannon fire, 1645. This eighteenth-century engraving simulates the start of the battle.

The Raw Dykes, an engraving published by William Stukeley in September 1722. The track on the right became Aylestone Road.

This engraving from a drawing published in 1722 by William Stukeley shows the site of the Raw Dykes where Prince Rupert assembled his cannon in 1645 to bombard the town of Leicester.

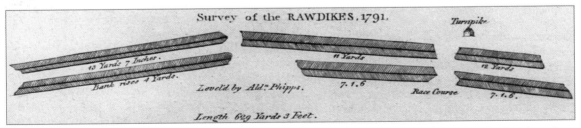

The remains of the Roman aqueduct constructed to carry clean water from the Wash Brook at Knighton into Ratae. The drawing was for a survey conducted by Richard Everard in the 1780s for John Throsby, the eighteenth-century local historian. Alderman Phipps, the owner of the land, destroyed much of the remaining aqueduct to accommodate a racecourse. It was from this embankment that Charles I directed his cannon against the town of Leicester.

The remains of the Raw Dykes, situated opposite the junction with Saffron Lane on Aylestone Road, 2003. A viewing platform is maintained by the Leicester City Council and the Dykes are well looked after.

The possible sight lines that Prince Rupert took on St Mary's Church Tower in 1645, from the embankment above the Raw Dykes. He fired his ranging shots at The Newarke. Today, Leicester City's football ground would obscure this line of fire.

St Mary's Tower, standing high above the Turret Gateway leading into the Leicester Castle courtyard. Modern historians have renamed this gateway Rupert's Archway, after the 1645 bombardment. The engraving was published in the 1860s. An engraving of Rupert's Tower is reproduced below.

The remains of the north front of Rupert's Tower on Bonners Lane in 1821, from a reproduction of a wood engraving by W. Burton.

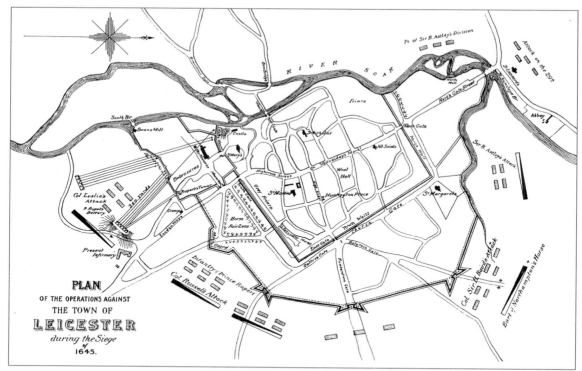

A plan of the siege of Leicester in 1645. This drawing was produced in 1839. Its accuracy is questionable. The drawing is based on the mid-nineteenth-century town.

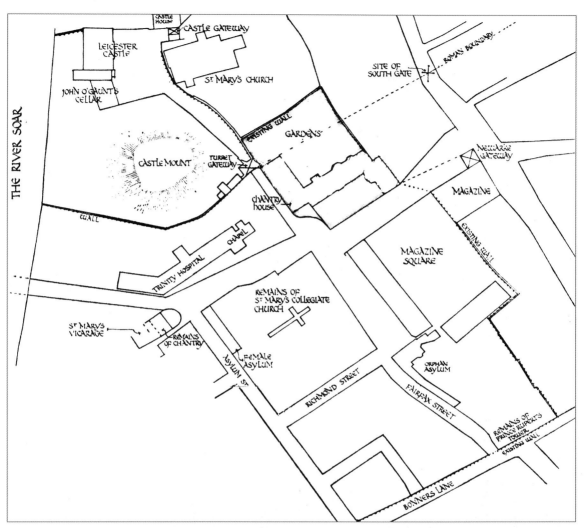

A plan produced in 1912 by students of the Leicester Municipal School of Art. These students conducted a survey on the surviving remains of The Newarke. On Bonners Lane the defensive wall survives, as do the remains of Prince Rupert's Tower. The defensive wall in the gardens of Chantry House is seen with its rifle embrasures. Unfortunately the remains of Rupert's Tower and the defensive wall on Bonners Lane were destroyed in the 1960s.

Opposite, bottom: The defensive wall in Chantry House gardens with the rifle embrasures, near the Turret Gateway to the Leicester Castle courtyard, July 2003.

A drawing by B.F. Scott of the defensive walls at the north-west corner of the castle mound, 1840. Evidence of repairs after the 1645 siege are clearly visible. Some of these remains may have survived at the base of the mound.

The principal breach of the defensive walls into The Newarke caused by Rupert's cannon, drawn in 1840 by B.F. Scott.

The defensive wall in Chantry House gardens with the rifle embrasures, July 2003. From Newarke House Museum this historic wall may be viewed from the garden.

The defensive wall that stood at the junction of Bonners Lane and Fairfax Street, *c.* 1880.

The Tudor gatehouse viewed from Leicester Castle courtyard, 1930s.

The turret gate leading into Leicester Castle courtyard, with the spire of St Mary's high in the background and Chantry House on the left, *c.* 1920.

The Newarke gateway and magazine, 1905.

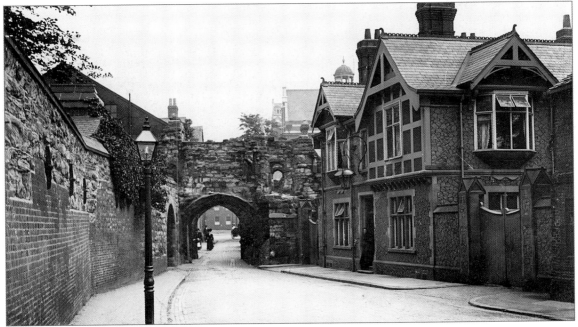

The Turret gateway viewed from the courtyard at Leicester Castle, *c.* 1920.

A wood engraving illustrating Leicester Abbey, *c.* 1840. It appears that parts of the ruins are occupied.

A similar view of Leicester Abbey, published in the 1930s.

The defensive walls at Leicester Abbey facing the town, with St Margaret's high to the left, *c.* 1790.

Defensive walls on the marshland near the River Soar at Leicester Abbey, *c.* 1790, an extremely fine defensive feature but hardly of any use for the defenders of the town, because the abbey was owned by Royalists.

Defensive rifle embrasures in the walls of
Leicester Abbey, July 2003.

Entrance to a defensive position on
Leicester Abbey walls, July 2003.

The ruins of Leicester Abbey, *c*. 1930. Charles I rested at Cavendish House, Leicester Abbey, during the siege of Leicester in 1645. The Countess of Devon lived at Abbey House. During the Civil War both Houses of Parliament gave instructions that she should be left alone. Henry Hastings burnt the house down while he was occupying the town to prevent Cromwell's troops using the premises.

The ruins of Leicester Abbey, from a wood engraving published in about 1840. In the background stands Cavendish House. From the illustrations and photographs on pp. 55 and 56 it was clearly an excellent defensive position, preventing any attempts on the king's life from the Parliamentarians occupying the town of Leicester.

Oliver Cromwell, Lord Protector 1653–8. Oliver, born in Huntingdonshire, was elected its MP and was well known for his passionate speeches against the king. He raised a troop of cavalry trained in the flat lands on the eastern fenland. He led his troops at the Battle of Edgehill in October 1642 and his rise through the Parliamentary army began. Cromwell became a supreme army commander under the brilliant leadership of Thomas Fairfax. Cromwell, to his credit, refused the crown of England. Could he foresee that a type of monarchy would return? Much of his rule was wrong, but through his ruthless approach to changing parliamentary laws, a true democracy commenced.

Huntingdon Tower, 1902. This important house stood on High Street and was also known as the Tower House, Lord Place, Reynolds Place and Huntingdon Place. The original Huntingdon Tower was built in about 1500; in 1565 it was owned by Richard Reynold. The original structure had two towers to the grand main entrance. Later it was owned by Henry, 3rd Earl of Huntingdon (1536–95). When Charles I visited Leicester in 1642 with Prince Rupert they were invited to stay at this splendid house. After the restoration of the monarchy, Charles II stayed at Huntingdon Place.

The Shires Tower, 2001. This splendid building was opened in 1991. The tower leads to a fine shopping complex. It is a shame that the local authority could not have erected a historic plaque to commemorate the fact that three kings stayed in a tower house that once stood near this tower: James I, Charles I and Charles II. Charles I was instrumental in starting the English Civil War through visiting Leicester and staying at Huntingdon Place in 1642. How many visitors who walk through the entrance to the Shires shopping complex are aware they are walking over deeply entrenched English history?

STOUGHTON

There were sixteen airfields built or maintained in Leicestershire to support the war effort. Castle Donington, Loughborough, Wymeswold, Melton Mowbray, Saltby, Bottesford, Ratcliffe, Rearsby, Desford, Leicester Municipal, Leicester East, Nuneaton, Bruntingthorpe, Market Harborough, Bitteswell and Husbands Bosworth. They would all have been defended by the RAF, the army or the Home Guard. How many retaliated against enemy attack or bombing raids? Very few. During the Second World War rigid censorship was essential; in many instances no records were retained. Anti-aircraft (AA) positions and sub-machine-gun emplacements were never accurately recorded. An AA battery was positioned off Anstey Lane near Gilroes cemetery; there is no available evidence that the guns were fired. There was a battery at Barkby with sub-machine-guns where they did open fire. A similar battery was erected just outside Stoughton, to the east of the village with a clear view of the church of St Mary. An attempt was made to bomb the area when Stoughton airfield, Leicester East, was being built, and the guns did open fire. These guns were replaced with replicas, and repositioned on the south coast to defend the D-Day landings into Europe. The AA battery site can still be located on a farm track, as indicated in this photograph from July 2003.

Stoughton airfield, built as Leicester East airfield and opened on 15 October 1943, seen here in 1998. It is doubtful that this took part in any battle. What is worth recording is that much has been retained of a Second World War airfield. Leicestershire Aero Club has repaired and now maintains much of the wartime site.

Part of the encircling perimeter track, 1998.

The Second World War control tower has been restored and is used by Leicestershire Aero Club, August 2003.

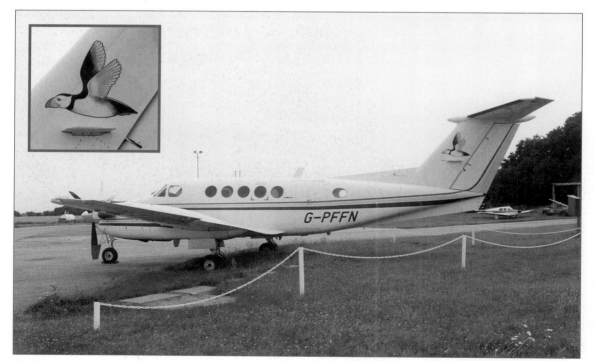

'Puffin' on the perimeter track near the control tower, August 2003. Farmland was requisitioned in 1940 to build this airfield, which had been planned as an aerodrome long before the Second World War. This site is part of Second World War history. The author recommends a visit to one of the many open days held here.

BARKBY

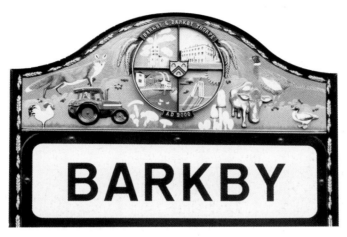

Welcome to Barkby. How many people realise that this is a Second World War battle site?

Kingfisher Bridge on the Barkby Brook, Main Street, July 2003. Just beyond the bridge on the right is the site of an army camp and AA gun site, long since cleared and returned to agriculture.

Part of Merton Farm where the AA gun site was erected in 1941. It may possibly have been built to defend the extensive Royal Ordnance Depot. This site was cleared and is now the modern village of East Goscote. On site three 3.7-inch AA guns were erected; these were fired on three occasions against overflying German aircraft, with no results. A Lewis-gun emplacement was also built on this site in January 1942. The double-sized magazines designed for anti-aircraft purposes held ninety-four rounds. This site was attacked with machine-gun fire by a German reconnaissance aircraft. The troops in charge of the Lewis gun replied, and according to comments from serving soldiers this aircraft crash-landed in Norfolk. Written confirmation was never produced because of wartime reporting restrictions.

The .303 light automatic gun, air-cooled, gas-operated, magazine-fed. Weight, 26–8lb. A normal magazine holds forty-seven rounds, but a double-sized magazine was available for the Barkby Lewis gun. Length of gun: 50.5 inches; length of barrel: 26.25 inches; velocity of bullets: 2,440 feet per second.

2
Bosworth & Religion

The Soldier's Widow. This engraving produced by A.H. Payne and published in the 1850s is a typical romantic picture from the Victorian period. It shows a cavalier, wounded in battle and left to die on the battlefield, found by his wife, a camp follower, who erected a simple screen to protect her dying husband. The poignant illustration records so much that is heartbreaking to families in wartime. This picture records the end of a battle during the English Civil War.

GILMORTON

All Saints' Church, Gilmorton, extensively rebuilt during the Victorian period, standing behind the motte and bailey fortification, August 2003. A footpath leads from the church across the castle site.

The site of Morton Castle. Morton was granted to Robert de Vessay by William I after the Battle of Hastings. De Vessay was granted considerable lands in the Midlands and sublet Morton to Godfrey, one of his junior knights, who brought over a number of his own servants and granted them areas of land. At the time of the great survey of 1086 'five Frenchmen' were causing considerable problems with the local Saxons who objected to foreign occupation of their farms. William Count de Harcourt, a leading knight and one of King William's loyal generals, was appointed in charge of Morton. It is possible that he commissioned the building of the motte and bailey castle to control the district and subdue the Saxons who objected to Norman rule and conducted a guerrilla war in this isolated area of the Midlands.

A drawing of Gilmorton Castle (known as Morton Castle when it was built), published in 1906. Morton was controlled by the Harcourt family for over 200 years. In 1257 when Richard Harcourt died the village had been called Gilmorton for many years, and it is referred to as such on today's Ordnance Survey maps.

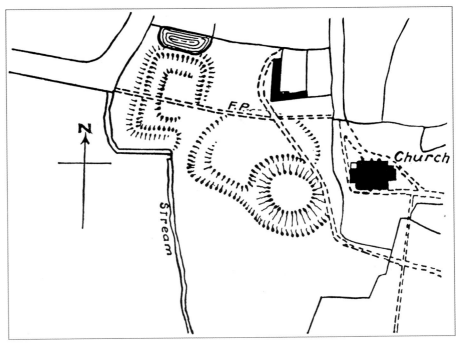

The remains of the moat that protected the bailey at Morton Castle, 2003. Bullrushes are in full flower. There are reasonable grounds to believe that a manor house was later built on this site, protected by the moat that also supported fish, particularly carp. They would have provided food for the table, similar to Kirby Muxloe Castle today (see p. 85).

HINCKLEY

When William the Conqueror defeated Harold the Saxon in 1066 on the battlefield in Sussex, he commenced the occupation and suppression of the indigenous population. After his coronation, he marched north through England with his knights. He transferred the ownership of every estate in Saxon hands to his Norman generals, making them directly responsible to the king. When unrest was apparent, motte and bailey castles were erected very quickly, in the most dominant position, with a ditch, mound, and palisade.

Earl Aubrey of Northumbria was granted Hinckley, one of the small estates in west Leicestershire, by the king in the early 1070s, and is recorded in the Domesday Book of 1086 as the landowner. Soon after this date the king became dissatisfied with Earl Aubrey; he could not control the local inhabitants and seemed incapable of erecting a castle, so he returned to Normandy.

When was the motte and bailey castle at Hinckley first erected? Certainly by 1068 the king was building castles at Warwick, Nottingham, Lincoln and Leicester, though not at Hinckley because of lack of cooperation by Aubrey. Various historians have put forward views on who built this castle. It is possible that the king authorised Hugh de Grantmesnil to build it. William I had granted him Leicester and extensive estates in Leicestershire and Warwickshire. Did Hugh de Grantmesnil maintain the castle until his death in 1098? During the years 1087 to 1093 he waged war against William Rufus (William II). During the baronial wars most castles were under siege. On Hugh's death his son, Aubrey de Grantmesnil, took up residence at Hinckley Castle. Through the reigns of Henry I, Henry II, Richard I, John, Henry III, Edward I and Edward II until the time of Edward III it would seem that the castle was fortified, partially demolished and occupied by a variety of noblemen in possession of the castle for the king. John of Gaunt then occupied the castle and restored it to its former glory. After his death it passed into the hands of Henry IV. It fell into disrepair, the stone was stolen for building projects in the town and by 1460 it had been completely destroyed.

The war memorial in the remains of Hinckley Castle, June 2003.

The site of Hinckley Castle, a plan based on the Ordnance Survey, 1906. Evidence of a deep water-filled moat survives. With such a depth of water surrounding the castle and with high stone walls it would have been very easy to defend.

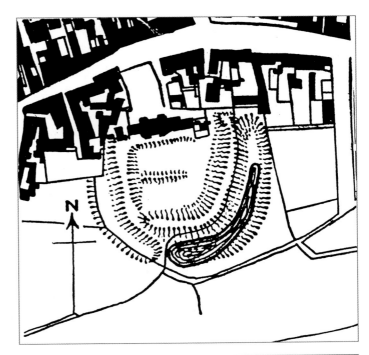

Part of the water-filled moat at Hinckley Castle, 2003.

The Garden of Remembrance in the centre of Hinckley Castle, 1930s.

The author and Jo Humberston sitting in the well-maintained garden at Hinckley Castle in 2003, part of the bailey in the original defensive system.

BOSWORTH FIELD

Much has been written about the Battle of Bosworth in recent years, because so little was recorded before and after the battle in 1485 and because after 1066 it was one of the most important changes in English history. The victor at Hastings introduced political change and was instrumental in recording Saxon England. The Tudors did the same after the Battle of Bosworth.

The two combatants were Richard III and Henry Tudor. History does not speak well of Richard III, frankly because the victor normally writes the history. Henry VII gained his throne by killing the king in battle: possibly Richard III got his just desserts. But Richard's image has been permanently tarnished by his supposed murder of his nephews, the 'princes in the tower'. Edward V became king in 1483 at the age of thirteen and reigned for seventy-seven days. Richard of Gloucester was appointed by Edward IV as the protector of his son. Richard, the uncle of Edward V, placed him in the Tower of London, a royal residence, for his safe keeping, along with his brother Richard. Richard of Gloucester declared the country a regency until Edward V reached his majority. He was not satisfied with this; the king and his brother went missing, having been declared bastards by the unscrupulous Bishop of Bath and Wells. Their putative remains, two skeletons, were uncovered in 1933. Possibly they were killed by either the Duke of Buckingham or the Earl of Richmond, but none of this has ever been conclusively proved.

King Richard III was a formidable warrior; a strong, unscrupulous leader during his short reign, he ruled England with a rod of iron and attempted to kill all his enemies. In 1482 his son died and his queen the year after. He ran the country with his hated lieutenants, Catesby, Ratcliffe and Lovell, under the flag of the wild boar. After the death of his wife, Richard proposed marriage to the sister of the missing princes Edward V and Richard, but died on Bosworth Field before this marriage could take place. Richard III had a force of approximately 8,000 men facing Henry Tudor's army of about 5,000 men. A balance of 3,000 was critical, because of the uncertainty of Lord Thomas Stanley's regiment. In an attempt to guarantee his support Richard had imprisoned Stanley's son on the understanding that if Thomas did not support him in battle, his son would be executed on site. At the commencement of the battle Stanley's regiment was held in reserve; eventually he supported Henry Tudor, a conclusive decision. His son had been released. Was this during the battle or after Henry had been crowned king by Lord Thomas Stanley? Richard III, whatever his shortcomings were, like many rulers before and since, 'he who lives by the sword shall die by the sword'! The king 'fell in the field, struck by many mortal wounds, a bold and valiant prince'.

The young Welsh upstart, crowned King of England on the battlefield, became King Henry VII. He fought one more battle to end this civil war, the Wars of the Roses, at Stoke Field on the River Trent a few miles north of the borders of Leicestershire. To consolidate the two warring factions, as a Lancastrian, he married Elizabeth of York, so uniting the two 'Roses'.

Edward V, the eldest son of Edward IV trained to be King of England from a very early age. He became Prince of Wales in 1471. Under the protection of his uncle, before the coronation could take place he was declared a bastard because his father had become engaged to marry Lady Eleanor Butler, but changed his

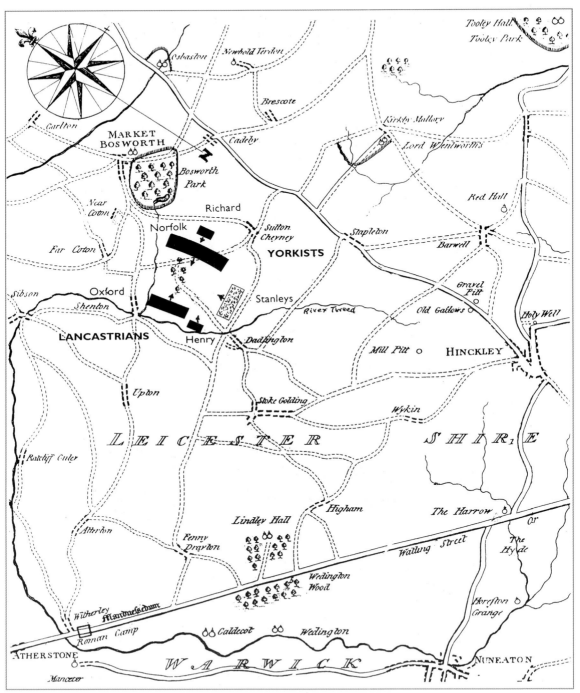

A plan of the Battle of Bosworth. This drawing was produced before the enclosure awards were finally completed for this area in 1794.

mind and married Elizabeth Woodville instead. According to the Bishop of Bath and Wells the betrothal to any woman was legally binding. Richard III became king in 1483, for approximately two years. Henry VII was king for twenty-four years. His son Henry VIII became king, and betrothal, marriage and divorce took on an entirely different meaning, when the Church of England was formed with his severance from Rome.

In 1785 J. Robinson produced a map of the area around Market Bosworth and Hinckley, during the completion of the enclosure awards concerning the open fields. He attempted to locate the Battle of Bosworth. Opposite is a section of Robinson's map. On this the author indicates modern observations, such as where the armies could have faced each other, before the battle started, to the north of Dadlington. Modern scholars offer conflicting views. From archaeological evidence that has been uncovered over past centuries, the site, as recorded by the Leicestershire County Council, is considered to be the approximate area of the main battle of 1485.

Engravings of spurs, spear heads, and a gold ring found in fields to the north of Dadlington in the middle of the eighteenth century.

Richard III, 1483–5, the last Plantagenet king. He was crowned through the efforts of the Duke of Buckingham who was later beheaded by Richard. These were tumultuous and terrible times when lives were cheap, including those of the royal family. The king with the strongest army held on to the throne throughout the medieval period, especially during the Wars of the Roses. Richard had learned his skill as a soldier during the terrible civil war between the Lancastrians and the Yorkists. He served with great courage in the Battles of Towton and Barnet in 1471 under his elder brother Edward IV, on whose death he challenged the right of his brother's eldest son, Edward V, to become king. Richard's very short reign ended at the Battle of Bosworth in Leicestershire and resulted in the change of the royal line, with the commencement of the Tudor dynasty.

An engraving published in the 1790s indicating two armies at the beginning of the Battle of Bosworth. It is a romantic illustration. There is some doubt that both armies had advanced so close before the first engagement that took place in the parish of Sutton Cheney.

Church of St James, Sutton Cheney, from an engraving produced in the 1790s. A church on this site was founded before 1100. When the enclosure awards of 1794 were enforced the highway that passed along the side of this church was removed. This was the route that Richard III's army used to get to the battle on Redmore Plain on 22 August 1485. Legend has it that the king attended his last Mass in this church on the same day.

Church of St James, spring 2000. In this church the annual memorial service to Richard III, the last English king to be killed in battle, is held on the Sunday nearest to 22 August.

Above: Legend has it that when Richard III passed this way with his army in 1485 his troops stopped to sharpen their swords on the sandstone corbel supports on this church. Grooves in the stone are still clearly in evidence.

Right: The brass memorial to Richard III surmounted with his coat of arms, in Sutton Cheney's church.

REMEMBER BEFORE GOD
RICHARD III
KING OF ENGLAND
AND THOSE WHO FELL
AT BOSWORTH FIELD
HAVING KEPT FAITH
22 AUGUST 1485

Loyaulté me lie

The site in Sandford where it is thought that the last king of England was killed in battle, photographed in 2003.

Four photographs from Saturday 16 August 2003 of the Battle of Bosworth re-enactment: camp followers; on parade; marching to battle; preparing to charge.

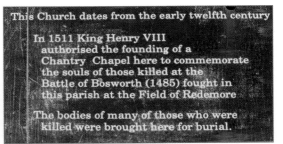

This Church dates from the early twelfth century

In 1511 King Henry VIII authorised the founding of a Chantry Chapel here to commemorate the souls of those killed at the Battle of Bosworth (1485) fought in this parish at the Field of Redemore

The bodies of many of those who were killed were brought here for burial.

Church of St James, Dadlington, June 2003.

Dadlington's small church is a thirteenth-century construction. This engraving was published in 1790. Considerable restoration took place in 1890. If this engraving is compared with the image above it can be seen that much of the early building has been lost, especially the half-timbered upper stage with a clerestory.

The Leicestershire artist/historian Rigby Graham visited Dadlington on 4 November 1975 and produced this drawing indicating the pub and the church while he was conducting an educational survey in the district.

The church of St James always excites historians seeking the history of the famous battle that took place to the north of this hamlet. Visit the church, then enjoy the hospitality at the public house situated near the church. Note the unusual pub name of the Dog and Hedgehog.

The cairn that was erected at the expense of Leicestershire historian Samuel Parr in 1813, seen here in 1905. According to local legend the well on this site is where Richard III quenched his thirst during the battle.

'King Dick's Well', 1904. Today a fence has been erected around this cairn and the well is maintained by the Fellowship of the White Boar. In the background, to the right, is the farmhouse that has been converted into the Bosworth battlefield visitors' centre.

The church of St John, Shenton. This engraving of the thirteenth-century church was published in 1790. The village at Shenton stands to the west of the battlefield and must have been involved, possibly by the troops serving as part of Oxford's regiment. See the map on p. 72.

Shenton's church of St John, June 2003. In 1859 the church seen above was considered to be beyond repair and it was thought impossible to preserve or restore the building. It was demolished. The present structure was built during 1860–1 by W.H. Knight, a contractor from Cheltenham. Very little of the historic past was retained.

BOSWORTH: ENGLISH CIVIL WAR

A romantic drawing of the road to Market Bosworth from Sutton Cheney, published in the 1840s.

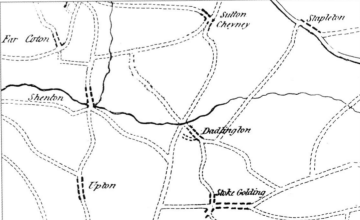

During the excavation of a ditch when the 1790s enclosure awards were being completed, this sword was found. It had been lost during the minor battle of 1644.

In 1644 a minor battle took place on Bosworth Field between Colonel Henry Hastings of Ashby and Lord Grey of Groby. It was a cavalry skirmish; 80 Parliamentary horse met 120 Cavaliers. Captain Thomas Babington under the direction of Lord Grey, charged. In the ensuing battle six of the king's men were killed and more than forty prisoners were taken. This conflict took place on the open fields north of Dadlington, then recorded as the site of the Battle of Bosworth.

KIRBY MUXLOE

The imposing bulk of Kirby Muxloe Castle. The original house was constructed as a fortified manor house by Robert Pakeman, and was subject to siege and defensive retaliation during the baronial wars of the thirteenth century. It was inherited by the Peverels, and eventually by William Herle, who was Chief Justice to Edward I. Herle's daughter married Ralph Hastings, who died in 1346.

The grand entrance to Kirby Muxloe Castle. The recent building was erected on the instructions of William Lord Hasting on the site of the original house, and the early stages of the old hall were incorporated into the present building. The original builder who supported Henry III died in 1271.

Remains of the west tower, 2003. The moat at Kirby Muxloe Castle has been well maintained over the centuries. Today large carp slowly swim around the moat and provide excellent fishing for the members of an exclusive fishing club.

Church of St Bartholomew, c. 1920. This church is thought to have been built in the 1290s under the direction of William Herle, a member of Edward I's court. Colonel Hastings's regiment passed this church on their way to besieging Leicester in 1645 and quartered their horses in the grounds of Kirby Muxloe Castle as a defensive position.

GROBY

The site of Groby Castle, an engraving published in the 1790s. In the background stands Old Hall, built from stone removed from the castle when it was partially demolished at the end of the twelfth century. This motte and bailey construction was one of the important castles built in Leicestershire on the instructions of William I by Hugh de Grantmesnil. The Saxon chief whose land he owned prior to the Conquest was Ulf of Markfield, one of the few Saxon landowners who, for a time, paid allegiance to William. It is fairly certain that Ulf took part in the abortive uprising with Earl Waltheof in 1075. During the reign of Stephen (1135–54) it is thought that a stone tower was erected in the centre of the motte, possibly from the remains of the Saxon church that stood nearby. This remote village was subject to many raids during those turbulent years.

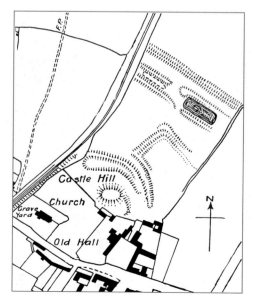

Groby Castle, 1906. In the 1140s Robert, Earl of Leicester, reinforced the castle, which passed into the hands of William de Ferrers. After the rebellion against Henry II, the king attacked and slighted the building on the defeat of the occupiers. In the 1590s the base of a stone tower on the mound near the church was still in situ.

Old Hall, on the Markfield Road to the east of the church of St Philip and St James. Thomas Grey of Groby built this hall from stone recovered from Groby Castle in the fifteenth century. This engraving was published in the 1790s and indicates ruined walls. Unrecorded stone walls still remain on the site. These may be defensive castle walls.

The three-storey tower of Old Hall, Groby that still stands, August 2003. It can easily be recognised in the engraving above, and possibly pre-dates the stone hall. Evidence of the arms of the de Ferrers is incorporated in the diapering on the tower.

WHITWICK CASTLE

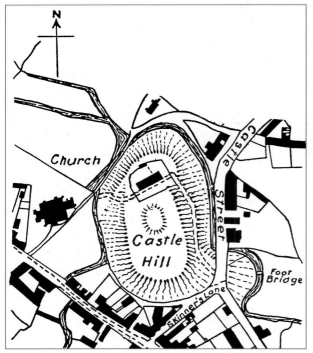

The remains of Whitwick Castle viewed from Castle Street, July 2003.

A plan of Whitwick Castle published in 1906. This castle was built in about 1075 as a result of the English uprising against the Normans of 1069–71. 'Witewic' was little more than a few houses on the edge of Charnwood Forest. This woodland provided excellent cover for Saxons who were involved in the revolt. This site is located on a natural hillock and is almost completely surrounded by two streams, tributaries of Grace Dieu Brook. These were easily dammed, so forming a superb moat, so it was a well-fortified castle. De Beaumont, Earl of Leicester, was in possession of the castle during the anarchy period of Stephen. In 1217 the Earl of Pembroke besieged the castle which was then under the ownership of Saer de Quency; he surrendered, and Pembroke slighted the walls. The building was rebuilt in 1320 when Edward II granted Henry de Beaumont permission to crenellate the castle. By 1427 the castle was described as 'old and ruinous'.

A tributary of Grace Dieu Brook to the north of the castle. The remains of the castle walls are clearly in evidence at the edge of the moat, July 2003.

Medieval faces carved in stone looking towards the castle from the church of St John the Baptist.

St John the Baptist Church with the castle mound in the background, *c*. 1790.

The war memorial to those lost in both world wars. It stands in front of the tower of St John the Baptist Church, July 2003.

3
Defence of the Realm

In this book much has been written about battles; this photograph illustrates a battle that did not take place, the invasion of Great Britain at the start of the Second World War. After Dunkirk, invasion by German forces from Europe appeared to be imminent. The initial attack would have been made across the English Channel into the southern counties of England. As the invasion was consolidated, air attacks and sea landings would have commenced into Lincolnshire across the North Sea.

In the 1940s forward planning was undertaken by the War Office and defensive positions were very quickly built throughout the countryside and of course in cities and towns. A common design was the quadrillage pillbox, developed during and after the trench warfare of the First World War: this was a simple design constructed from reinforced concrete.

This pillbox still standing on the hillside to the south of Stathern in February 2004 was built in a strategic position overlooking the Vale of Belvoir. It was an excellent observation post and defensive position. In the latter half of 1941 extensive permanent fortifications had been built throughout the British Isles. From the Humber to the Thames, along the North Sea coastline were built continuous concrete fortifications, coastal gun forts. From the Thames along the south coast to Southampton on 'Invasion Corner' an extensive concentration of assorted batteries was erected. Today, where these small forts survive, they are a permanent record of one of the darkest periods of the history of the British Isles.

MOUNTSORREL CASTLE

Mountsorrel Castle viewed from the Soar Valley, *c.* 1910.

A castle was built on this hill by Hugh Lupus, Earl of Chester, in about 1085 to control the river valley north of Leicester. It was in the possession of the Earls of Leicester from about 1140. During the reign of Stephen it withstood numerous attacks during the baronial wars. In the period 1173–4 it was held by Prince Henry who was in revolt against his father Henry II, who took the castle after a lengthy siege. Richard I fortified the building and built an extensive tower and hall from local stone. The castle came under the control of Saer de Quincy against King John during the barons' war of 1215; in 1217 William Marshall, Earl of Pembroke, besieged the castle on behalf of Henry III. The castle was held by a group of baronial mercenaries under the leadership of Ranulf, Earl of Chester. After the Battle of Lincoln in 1217, the king ordered this castle to be destroyed, describing it as 'a nest of the Devil and a Den of Thieves'.

Richard I, son of Henry II.

Castle Hill, Mountsorrel, is worth visiting. Here a group of visitors stands in the cupola built in 1793, below the castle site.

The First World War memorial, designed by Shirley Harrison, was erected on the site of Mountsorrel Castle in 1926. This Leicestershire battle site is well worth visiting on a sunny summer day, to enjoy the views and attempt to understand the importance of this site in the baronial wars of the twelfth and thirteenth centuries, and the seventeenth-century Civil War.

Exposed Mountsorrel granite was extensively mined in the area. Natural stone was used in the construction of the original castle. Stone masons employed by Richard I reinforced the existing castle. Carefully laid granite floors can still be found in the grassed areas of the ruined castle, August 2003.

The beacon, Mountsorrel Castle, with visitors, August 2003. After the young king gave instructions in 1217 to the Earl of Pembroke, his guardian, to demolish this castle, the stone was plundered and mining took place in and near the bailey.

The monument and commemorative plaque to William Marshall, Earl of Pembroke, guardian to Henry III, who succeeded to the throne at the age of nine. This powerful earl ran the country on his behalf, from 1216 to 1219.

WILLIAM MARSHALL, EARL OF PEMBROKE, WHO LED THE UNSUCCESSFUL BESIEGING FORCE ON MOUNTSORREL CASTLE, 1217, ON BEHALF OF THE KING. THE SIEGE WAS LIFTED WHEN THE KING'S MEN WERE THREATENED BY THE COMBINED FRENCH AND BARONIAL ARMY.

The remains of Mountsorrel Castle in the 1790s. In March 1643 Royalists used this as a defensive position during a skirmish. Hastings's troops from Ashby de la Zouch fought through the village with a Roundhead force from Leicester and retreated to the ruined castle.

The Green, Mountsorrel, c. 1910. Royalists controlled the village in 1643 from their defensive position on the castle site; skirmishes took place on the village green.

LOUGHBOROUGH – THE LUDDITES

Wright's Mill in Market Street, the site of John Heathcote's factory, 1980s. Formerly Mill Street, Market Street was the site of the only major skirmish involving Luddite workers in the eighteenth and nineteenth centuries in Leicestershire.

Market Street, Loughborough, November 2003. On 28 June 1816 a mob of 100 men with blackened faces charged down Mill Street and smashed their way into John Heathcote's lace factory, armed with pistols. They shot and wounded one of the armed factory watchmen, John Asher; nine others surrendered. The men then destroyed all the lacemaking machines. Eventually eight men from the mob were apprehended. Their leader James Towle and four others were hanged at Leicester gaol in April 1817, the remaining three were transported. Heathcote sold up and set up his business in Devon.

COTES BRIDGE

On the ancient highway now known as the A60 stands Cotes Bridge. In prehistoric times the River Soar would have been forded at the present site. Possibly the first bridge had been built of wood by 1086 to serve the two Saxon mills that had been erected nearby. The hamlet of Cotes was granted by King Ethelred (978–1016) as part of the parish of Prestwold. This bridge stands at an important road junction on the highway and would have featured in many movements of troops around the countryside.

The present bridge has been extensively changed over the last two centuries. From the engraving published in 1793 and seen on p. 98 it appears that the bridge consisted of thirteen arches. The Soar was divided into four channels at this point. The bridge was half a mile in length and extremely narrow, a classic packhorse bridge. Supporting arches were built on three of the small islands standing on the flood plain. During the winter months, passage along the highway would not have been possible without this long bridge. Low supporting walls were constructed along the line of the causeway.

Unquestionably a most important battle took place at this bridge on the Nottingham to Loughborough road. This was as a result of a skirmish on 16 March 1643 with Hastings's troops from Ashby de la Zouch and Roundheads from Leicester, at Mountsorrel. Royalists were forced into a defensive position on Castle Hill in the village, and they then controlled the Loughborough road. From this position they set up defensive earthworks at Cotes Bridge allowing the Royalists to control a considerable length of an important highway. Taking up these positions on 17 March, fighting and skirmishing continued for three days until the 20th.

This small battle came about because of more important campaigns in the Civil War. Troop movements required clear and open roadways. Sir Charles Lucas and Hastings – Lord Loughborough – were marching with their troops from Oxford to Newark along the highway via Cotes Bridge, which was secured by Royalist troops from Ashby de la Zouch. To prevent the Royalists marching north, Sir Edward Hartopp marched from Leicester with Lord Grey's regiment. Battle commenced at the bridge. The Parliamentarian contingent was armed with three cannon, which were set up on the Melton Mowbray side of the river, under the direction of Artilleryman Russell; extensive use of grapeshot cleared the bridge. The Roundheads charged and secured the bridge. The Royalists retreated into their prepared trenches, so a stalemate developed. Controlled trench warfare requires time. The five lines of trenches that had been dug on the Loughborough side of the river were impregnable and could only be taken through sapping the lines with extensive movements of advancing earthworks. On the 20th the Parliamentarians retreated; they had been warned that Prince Rupert was advancing on this position with 2,000 cavalrymen from the east. They would have been trapped on the bridge, so a retreat back to Leicester was ordered, and so ended the Battle of Cotes Bridge.

Cotes Bridge, 1793. In the background of this engraving stands Lower Cotes watermill. The thirteen arches over the Soar made a causeway with other small connecting bridges across the marshes leading to Loughborough.

Cotes Bridge watermill, *c.* 1890. This would certainly have been used as an observation position, probably by the Royalist forces. Two watermills existed near the bridge during the conflict that took place in 1643.

March 30th, 1644. — George Palmer, Captain Lieutenant to Colonell Thornhaugh, examined, sayth that upon Saterday, the 16th of March instant, this examinant comanded the forlorne hope wch was sent out by Order from Sr Edward Hartopp against the enemies then being about Mountsorrell, wch order was to that effect : That this examinant with the forlorne hope should goe to a certaine hill neere to Mountsorrell, there to make a stand untill the rest of the bodie of the pliament side come up ; whereupon the enemye beinge betwixt the hill & this examinant, this examinant seeing the enemie plunderinge horses from plowmen in the field, there fell uppon them, tooke three prisoners and forcd the other backe, and soe came to the hill. Then Sr Edward sent word to this examinant that he went too fast for the bodie to followe, and this examinant, hearinge by Scouts sent before that the enemye was squandered and dispiersed in the towne, went on and pursued the enemye. Then Sr Edward sent againe to make a stand, wch this examinant did. Then this examinants scouts cominge in brought intelligence, and likewise this Examinant hearde by some townsmen of Mountsorrell and others that the enemye was in their quarters in divers townes thereabouts, and divers of their foote dranke in Mountsorrell, whereupon this Examite sent Sr Edward notice thereof, desiringe to knowe whether he should fall on or not, and desiringe some asystance from him ; but this Examinant was Comanded by Captayne Innis in Sr Edwards name to march hard by the townes side and there to stand ; then the Enemye, perceiving their Comminge, drewe as manye as they could get together for the present into Battalia to face them in the meadowe betwixt them and the Enemye. Then, by Order of Capt. Ennys, this Examinant charged the enemye with the forlorne hope, and forced them to retreat over a bridge ; and, the enemy facing about, the forlorne hope rid forciblye over the bridge, and forced them backe into Mountsorrell. Then Sr Edward Hartopp, cominge up wth the bodie, stood looking upon them of the forlorne hope, but would send them noe reliefe, although sent to for it ; wch the Enemye pceiving sent reliefe to their bodye and soe beat this Examinant and the forlorne hope backe ; whereat the troops of Collonell Thornhays regiment were ready to mutinye upon sight thereof, and sayd they would not suffer this Examinant to be soe ingaged in their sight. Then came up a Lincolnshire troop without Order, as they sayd to relieve this Exam^t, when they were beaten backe by the enemy into the towne ; but being yet too weake, the enemy, seeing noe more helpe come, cut of divers of the forlorne hope and tooke manie prisoners and rescued their men prisoners taken from them, wch were considerable for number and qualitie. Then this Exam^t, being tyred in fight, went to Sr Edward and desired some reliefe, tellinge him their extremitye ; but he answered this Exam^t asking what authoritye this Exam^t had to goe over the bridge into the towne, and told this exam^t that a counsell of warre should goe on him and them y^t seconded him ; then this Exam^t, urging him for a fresh horse, he sayd he had none for this Exam^t, whereupon this Exam^t told Major Sanders thereof, who much grieved thereat helped this exam^t to a fresh horse, wherewith this Exam^t, cominge to Sr Edward for Orders, he Comanded all should retyre. Yet notwithstandinge, this Exam^t wth a Company of dragoons charged the enemye againe into the towne, and so brought of most of his men and kept the towne. Then Sr Edward sent Order againe that all the horse & dragoons should retire agayne, although they were very secure, being baracadoed wth Carts in the towne ; and soe they left it with great store of provisions of the enemyes wch they had taken from them, whereby they lost their qrter and provision there & were forced to be all night w^thout provision for horse or men. The next daye, being Saboath daye, some of the Notingham troopes told Sr Edward in the Exam^ts hearinge y^t if he would not suffer them to fight they would goe home, who answered that he had no Comission to fight, and if their Collonell was there he would hange up some of them for being soe forward, and soe passed from them. The next daye, when the fight was at Cotes bridge, and the foote ingaged in fight wth the enemye, this Exam^t went to Sr Edward for Orders to assyst them, but Sr Edward sent this Exam^t & Nottingham troops to the toppe of Stanford hill, there to stand untill further Order from him wch they had none untill they were comanded to retire after the fight was done.   GEORGE PALMER.

This examynation was taken before us, and is offered to be justified by the oathe of the Examinate.

THO. BABINGTON.
THO. HESILRIGE.
FR. SMALLEY.
WILL. STANLEY.

The translation of a report published by Alice Dryden in 1911 of the examination of Captain George Palmer taken in Leicester on 30 March 1644 by Tho. Babington, Tho. Hesilrige, Fr. Smalley and Will. Stanley of the Leicester Committee of Sequestrations. The document is now held at the County Record Office at Wigston.

A silver portrait badge of Charles I, shown larger than actual size, *c.* 1645. His loyal supporters displayed such badges during many of the military campaigns.

Lower Cotes Mill, 1930. Upper Cotes Mill was destroyed in 1898 to relieve flooding. Lower Cotes Mill ceased grinding corn for human consumption in the 1950s; it continued to grind animal foodstuff until 1973. Throughout the period of the English Civil War there was a dispute with the controlling landlords on the use of these two mills to grind corn.

The author with Jo Humberston inside Cotes Bridge watermill, now a pleasant restaurant, June 2004.

Cotes Bridge, 1991. There is evidence that some of the ancient stone bridge has been retained in the modern structure. The remains of a weir are still visible.

The modern brick bridge seen in 1991 when the River Soar was low. A causeway of stone and the support of the original medieval bridge is just visible through the clear water.

COLEORTON

Coleorton Hall, *c.* 1910. This was built between 1804 and 1808 on the site of the original hall, put up in the seventeenth century. During the Civil War it was occupied by the Hastings family of Ashby de la Zouch. Parliamentary troops from Derby and Nottingham attacked the defended hall in the autumn of 1644. Owing to the weight of numbers, Hastings's troops retreated to Ashby de la Zouch Castle.

Coleorton Hall, July 2003. In November 1644 Colonel Temple's Parliamentary troops, now garrisoned at Coleorton Hall, trained their cavalry on the park in front of the hall where these cattle stand today. Rather optimistically they attacked the nearby town of Ashby de la Zouch, where they won some provisions and took away some loaded carriages. In December they attacked again, while Henry Hastings was away. They sacked the town but could not make any impression on the well-defended castle.

BREEDON-ON-THE-HILL

This natural defensive position is situated in north-west Leicestershire, and evidence has been found there of the remains of axes used by Neolithic man some 3,000 years ago. Iron Age remains have also been uncovered in the Bulwarks. During the first century BC impressive ditches were dug around the perimeter, with palisades of sharpened tree trunks erected on the mounds inside the ditches. Round houses thatched with straw were put up inside the palisade and evidence has been uncovered on archaeological digs of pottery, hammerstones and querns. For some 200 years before the Roman occupation Breedon Hill was a defensive position and unquestionably was subjected to attack during the Iron Age period. It was defended against the Roman advance north through the country, and from evidence that has been uncovered it withstood Roman attack and eventually surrendered or came to terms with the Roman occupiers, who then developed it as a fortified settlement. Eventually a Roman villa was built, part of the agricultural development of the area, less than a mile south of the hill.

When the Romans left, the hill was maintained as a religious shrine. The local Celts associated natural features with supernatural forces and continued to pray to their gods on this site. In the fifth century AD the Anglo-Saxon occupation of this area of Leicestershire began. They had their own gods. As the Saxons controlled the area so Christianity re-established itself in England via Ireland and Iona. Penda the pagan Saxon king controlled Mercia from 577 to 655; on his death Ethelred became king and was converted to Christianity, financing the building of Breedon monastery in 676. Ethelred ruled Mercia from 655 until 704 when he became a monk, dying in 716. The defence of the monastery commenced with the rebuilding of the defensive fortifications of the Bulwarks with stone walls. In 874 the Danish army advanced into north Leicestershire, and after an attempt to defend the monastery the monks fled. Evidence exists that after the occupying Danes were converted to Christianity they restored part of the monastery, possibly the church, that they had earlier sacked. Saxon remains have been located throughout the church of St Mary and St Hardulph. Religion and peace descended on this fortified hill, though it was probably used as an observation point during the Wars of the Roses. It was not until the Civil War of the seventeenth century that further conflict involving this remarkable site occurred.

During April 1644 a temporary garrison was erected on Breedon Hill by Parliamentary troops from Derby and Leicester. Hastings's men from Ashby de la Zouch Castle were unaware of this – where were their local spies? Three hundred troops of cavalry and foot soldiers were marching north from Oxford to reinforce the Royalist army at Newark, along the highway south of Breedon. The troops from Breedon ambushed the Royalist regiment, killed eight soldiers, wounded many and took sixty prisoners. The Royalists lost this minor battle and fled to the safety of Ashby de la Zouch Castle.

The Bulwarks, Breedon-on-the-Hill, viewed from the village green, *c.* 1910.

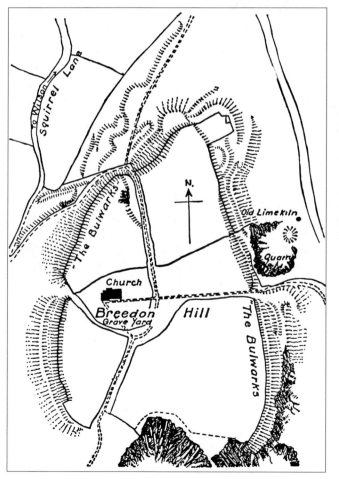

The crenellated tower of St Mary and St Hardulph Church, viewed from the east below the escarpment, July 2003.

The hill fortification, Breedon Hill, 1906.

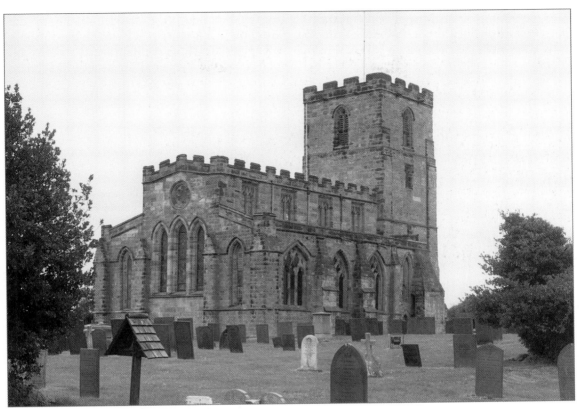

St Mary and St Hardulph Church, July 2003.

The beacon erected on Breedon Hill to
commemorate Queen Elizabeth II's Golden
Jubilee in 2002.

Anglo-Saxon carvings in St Mary and St Hardulph Church are considered to be one of the finest collections in Europe. When visiting this fine church you must purchase the guide book, study it carefully and then view all the carvings and splendid medieval monuments that are on display. Certainly the Saxon carvings are not displayed in their original positions. They were damaged during the Danish occupation, replaced during the rebuilding of the church and have been subjected to more recent vandalism.

Far left: The Breedon angel, carved in about 800.

Left: This splendid carving is at the end of the south aisle. A Byzantine blessing is being given.

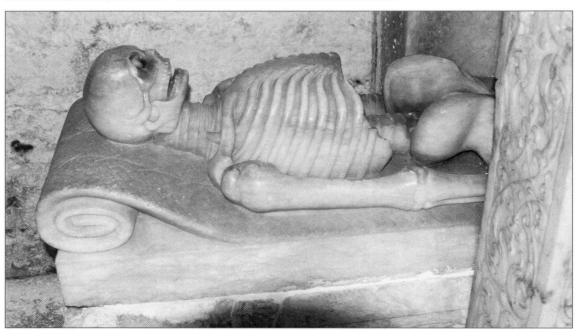

Beneath a display of carved columns lies this medieval gisant – a reclining figure atop its tomb.

KING'S MILLS

The Royalist commander, Henry Hastings, positioned a garrison of troops at King's Mills by the ferry on the River Trent. In January 1643, to consolidate his domination of south Derbyshire, north Leicestershire and parts of Nottinghamshire, Hastings had erected a fort on the island created in the system of watermills. A watermill is recorded on this site in the Domesday survey of 1086. At the end of the nineteenth century five mills were in operation, grinding corn, gypsum and making paper. Iron forging was also undertaken. When Hastings constructed his defensive position there he had considerable natural resources.

The river was deep enough at this point to maintain a quay. A ferry was already there to cross the Trent and bridges were built to serve this industrial centre from the east. Hastings appointed Captain Thomas Robinson as governor at King's Mills, and built a defensive position around the island with outworks of wooden palisades. From this defensive position he raided the surrounding countryside for food and ambushed small parties of foraging Parliamentarian troops. This annoyed Sir John Gell at his headquarters in Derby. On 6 February Gell assembled a large regiment of troops and surrounded both banks of the Trent. With a large troop of horse soldiers he prevented Hastings' Cavaliers from Ashby de la Zouch Castle relieving the outpost at King's Mills. A combined force of foot soldiers and cavalry charged the position. Unfortunately the defensive position had been depleted by Hastings for improving the defences at his castle. The cannon was light, the attacking Parliamentarian troops climbed the palisades, and one was killed and six were fatally wounded. The battle inside the defensive position was furious and successful. The fort was stormed and the occupants surrendered. In the final attack twenty Parliamentarians were wounded, some fatally, and five were killed. The occupying force amounted to the governor, one lieutenant and fifty-two soldiers; over twenty were killed or died of their wounds.

This engraving, published in 1790, gives a good impression of how King's Mills was positioned on the river. The hill on the right was covered in trees during the battle of 1643; it is on record that the attacking Parliamentarians slid down this hill into the defensive positions at the bottom. Visit King's Mills today, walk around the site along the footpaths and enjoy the common land. You can understand how it was very easy to defend. The tower of the fort, called 'the Priest House', still stands. Modern buildings have been constructed adjacent to the old fort and now form a splendid hotel, The Priest House on The River. It serves fine food and benefits from a beautiful situation.

King's Mills and the fortifications, *c.* 1790. The latter protected the river crossing and defended the corn mills, so important in the production of food for the controlling landowner.

The ferry at King's Mills on the River Trent, *c.* 1906.

On the footpath towards the Trent on the Nottinghamshire side, with the fortress in the background, *c.* 1910.

The ferry road leading to the Trent in front of the Fort, *c.* 1920.

An island bridge on the industrial site at King's Mills, with the workers' cottages on the right, *c.* 1915.

One of the watermill wheels that have been preserved on site at this industrial complex, July 2003. It was possibly the most important site of watermills producing flour and other products in Leicestershire, and closed down in 1927 after a disastrous fire.

The remains of a fort built on this site for protection and to prevent the unlawful crossing of the River Trent from Nottinghamshire to Leicestershire. How much of the original construction has now been incorporated into the Priest House Hotel after the battle in the Civil War is unknown. This photograph was taken in July 2003.

DONINGTON HALL

A mansion house was built on the site of the existing hall in the fourteenth century and was in the ownership of Thomas Plantagenet, Earl of Leicester, in 1310. During the turbulent times of the Wars of the Roses and eventually the Civil War it was attacked, abandoned and allowed to fall into ruin. Between 1790 and 1793 the old hall was demolished and a magnificent new one was built by William Wilkins in the style called Strawberry Hill Gothic. In the First World War it became a prisoner-of-war camp for captured German officers, clearly pictured in this photograph of about 1915.

German prisoners of war being escorted to Donington Hall. Two German officers escaped from this camp by tunnelling under the walls and wire. Today Donington Hall is the headquarters of British Midland Airways.

CASTLE DONINGTON

Market Street, Castle Donington, 1905. Known as Donitone in Domesday Book, 'Castle' was added to the name sometime after the castle was erected on the hill in the twelfth century.

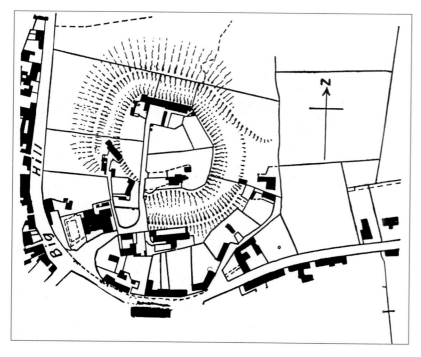

A plan of the castle at Castle Donington, published in 1907. This castle with its medieval keep was built at Donington in about 1135 by Eustace, Baron of Haulton during the reign of Stephen. During his turbulent reign it was attacked many times. It passed into the hands of Haulton's son, then through marriage it passed to John Lacy, one of the barons who opposed King John. The king attacked the castle in 1216, and it was taken after a lengthy siege. King John gave instructions for the castle to be demolished.

This engraving by John Cary from a drawing by John Pridden in July 1792 shows the remains of the castle. It was rebuilt by Henry Laci, Earl of Lincoln, who died in 1310. Thomas, Earl of Leicester, inherited the castle, but he was executed in 1322 and Edward II gave it to Hugh le Despensers. After the king was murdered the castle came into the hands of Edmund, Earl of Kent, who was executed in 1330; it passed to his son, eventually to Henry IV and then Henry V. During the Wars of the Roses it was held by the Lancastrians and granted to Sir William Hastings. It fell into decay and in 1595 Sir George Hastings preferred his more important castle at Ashby de la Zouch and gave instructions for it to be demolished, for the building stone.

The remains of one of the walls of the castle, situated on the footpath to a row of cottages to the north of the castle site, July 2003.

CASTLE DONINGTON AIRFIELD

Nottingham East Midlands airport, July 2003. A small Home Defence landing ground was set up in 1916, and used by 38 Squadron for about eighteen months. By 1941 RAF Castle Donington was on the site. It was officially opened in January 1943 and was closed down in September 1946. On 9 March 1964 the building of East Midlands airport began on the disused Second World War site.

Thousands of people pass through Nottingham East Midlands airport every month. How many of them realise that it was an active Second World War airfield used by the RAF? On 13 August 1941 the German air force attacked the new airfield, dropping twelve high-explosive bombs a few yards from the new runway. On 25 June 1942 another attack was made when 500 incendiaries were dropped – no doubt aimed at the fuel storage area. The RAF regiment fired back at the attacking German aircraft.

CASTLE DONINGTON AIRPORT MUSEUM

One way to appreciate the history around East Midlands airport is to sit in the Aeropark off the Castle Donington road, take a picnic, view the military aircraft on display and watch the variety of aircraft leaving the airport. This photograph was taken from the raised embankment in the Aeropark in July 2003.

The famous Vulcan on display in the Aeropark.

An RAF rescue helicopter, one of the many historic military aircraft on display at the Aeropark, July 2003.

ASHBY DE LA ZOUCH

In 1086 at the time of the Domesday survey 'Ascebi' had been granted to Hugh de Grantmesnil by William the Conqueror. On the site of the present castle he built a unfortified manor house from wood. Philip de Beaumont replaced the early manor house with a stone building in the 1150s. His subtenant lived in the manor house and was possibly related to the owner of the manor and surrounding

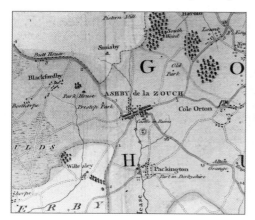

estate, Robert Belmeis. This family eventually held Ashby for the crown. In about 1160 the male Belmeis line died out and the manor of Ashby passed through a daughter to Alan la Zouch, a Breton nobleman. Through at least two generations this family extended their interest in the manor of Ashby. In 1219 it is recorded that a market was held in the town. At this time Ashby acquired the suffix 'de la Zouch'. The male heirs of the Zouch estate had died out by 1314, and it passed by marriage to Sir William Mortimer, created Baron Zouch of Ashby in 1323. What influence did Roger Mortimer, the lover of the French queen Isabella, wife of the weak Edward II, have on this appointment? Roger Mortimer had the king killed at Berkeley Castle. In 1330 his son Edward III, with friends, seized the murdering dictator at nearby Nottingham Castle. He was quickly conveyed to the gallows at the Tower of London.

In about 1326 Baron Zouch began converting the manor house into a defended castle. Did he consider he needed to defend his position as a baron and major landowner in north Leicestershire? Especially as a member of his family, Sir Roger la Zouch of Ashby, had been involved in the murder of Sir Roger de Beler, the king's commissioner, near Rearsby in January 1326. Edward III sought revenge for the death of Sir Roger on behalf of his widow (see p. 161). On the death of Baron Zouch, Alan la Zouch inherited the castle and estate and proceeded to extend the building in 1347. For the next fifty years the Zouch family continued to add to the castle and consolidated their estates in Leicestershire. In 1399 Hugh la Zouch died leaving no heirs. Ashby de la Zouch then changed ownership several times. It came into the hands of James Butler, Earl of Ormonde, a Lancastrian who was captured at Towton in the Wars of the Roses. Edward IV declared him a traitor in 1461, and had him beheaded. The castle and all the estates reverted to the crown, and Edward then granted the manor and castle to his Lord Chamberlain, William, Lord Hastings, in October 1464. Hastings, a shrewd politician and soldier, supported Edward IV in the Wars of the Roses, as has been seen. He rose rapidly in the Yorkist court and in 1474 the king granted Hastings licence to extend and build castles at Ashby and Kirby Muxloe. At his castle at Ashby he further extended the house within the protective walls but, above all, he gave instructions to build the Hastings Tower, a remarkably strong construction, with no windows at ground level and extremely thick walls at its base. Wells were dug in situ, completing an excellent defensive structure. On the death of his patron Edward IV, Richard, Duke of Gloucester, had Hastings beheaded in June 1483, a few days before Richard III was crowned king. Richard started to pick off the many barons he considered opposed him. The Wars of the Roses was reaching its climax, and Hastings's son supported the winning side at Bosworth Field.

For the next century and a half, the Hastings family prospered at Ashby de la Zouch. Royal visits to the castle were recorded: Henry VII in 1503; James I in 1614; Charles I and his Queen in 1634; Anne of Denmark and Prince Henry in 1683; but a much less willing incumbent, Mary Queen of Scots, in 1569 and 1586. Unquestionably the English Civil War was the most stirring time in the history of Ashby de la Zouch Castle. Hastings's eldest son succeeded to the title of Earl of Huntingdon in 1643, and took no part in the Civil War. His brother, the youngest son, became the chief protagonist of Charles I's cause. A leading officer in the king's army, after the Battle of Edgehill he occupied the castle, enlisting and training a strong army in the grounds. For over three years it became the centre for operations led

A colourwash of the castle produced by Charles Ashdown in 1915. The Hastings Tower is clearly visible.

by Henry Hastings's troops for most of Leicestershire, Nottinghamshire, Derbyshire and Staffordshire. Several improvements were made to the defensive systems, not least the building of underground passages between all the inner defensive structures. Henry Hastings was created Baron Loughborough and in February 1643 he was made colonel general. Many of the minor battles and skirmishes in Leicestershire involved Hastings or his troops, but by the end of 1644 the Parliamentary forces were gaining the upper hand. The town of Ashby de la Zouch was attacked and occupied by Parliamentary troops. The castle was besieged and subjected to continuous bombardment; the underground tunnels proved a godsend. After the Battle of Naseby the castle came under constant assault, but the attacking forces could not break down the castle defences. Food became scarce and the diseased, injured and weak troops decided they had had enough. On 28 February 1646 they negotiated an acceptable surrender, to the relief of the besieging force. Certainly the Hastings Tower of 1474 had proved its worth even with seventeenth-century cannon.

Lord Loughborough was a dashing Cavalier; his actions at war are too lengthy to include in this book. He lost an eye at a skirmish near Bardon, and he always led from the front with his sword raised high, a black patch over his eye, a terrible charging figure held in awe by his opponents. Parliament classed him as one of the great delinquents. Certainly he would have been executed, but he escaped from Windsor Castle in 1648. He joined Charles II in Holland, and on the restoration he was appointed Lord Lieutenant of Leicestershire. He died a bachelor in January 1667 and as a great Cavalier the king had him buried in St George's Chapel at Windsor.

The castle in 1730 from an engraving after Samuel and Nathaniel Buck. The building with a pitched roof in the centre of the engraving is still occupied at this time.

A view of the castle from the tower of the church of St Helen's, *c.* 1910.

The chapel in Ashby de la Zouch Castle from the west, 1905.

A southern view of the chapel in Ashby de la Zouch Castle, *c.* 1910.

A fifteenth-century fireplace in the solar at the side of the main hall at Ashby de la Zouch Castle, 2003.

Impressive fifteenth-century fireplace in Ashby de la Zouch Castle, 2003. After the castle was slighted and made untenable on the instructions of Parliament, the Hastings family moved to nearby Donington Hall.

A coat of arms high up on the castle wall.

One of the wells inside the castle walls.

The south-east tower built in the 'wilderness' in the sixteenth century.

The south-west tower, a defensive structure in the sixteenth-century garden.

Schoolgirls from the nearby school who enacted a sequence of Chinese dances in the grounds of Ashby de la Zouch Castle in 1904.

The priest's room, Ashby de la Zouch Castle, 1910.

A view from the top of the Hastings Tower with Georgina and Beverley Grech standing in front of the chapel walls, August 2003.

The Hastings Tower, July 2003.

The tower of the church of St Helen's viewed through a window of the ruined castle, July 2003.

St Helen's Church, *c.* 1910. Built on the site of an earlier church on the instructions of William, Lord Hastings, in 1474. It was completed, after his execution in 1483, by his son. Amazingly this church suffered very little damage during the English Civil War.

4
Markets at War

An engraving of the manor house built on the site of Belvoir Castle, published in the 1790s.
The escarpment surrounding the castle has very few trees, still recovering from the Civil War attacks and defence. In 1646 the 8th Earl of Rutland hoped to save his castle. He supported the Parliamentary cause, but did not take up arms himself against the king. Cromwell did not appreciate this, and in 1649 instructed that the defensive building of Belvoir Castle must be destroyed. In 1654 the earl was allowed to rebuild a mansion house, not a castle, on the site.

NORMANTON

The main road looking north through Normanton, with Winthorpe House on the right and Three Shires Farm on the left, 1910. During the Second World War when Bottesford airfield was in full use there was no public highway through the village; see the plan opposite.

Bottesford aerodrome, on the road from Normanton to the village of Long Bennington. On the left-hand side are concrete feeder roads and an RAF hangar left over from the Second World War.

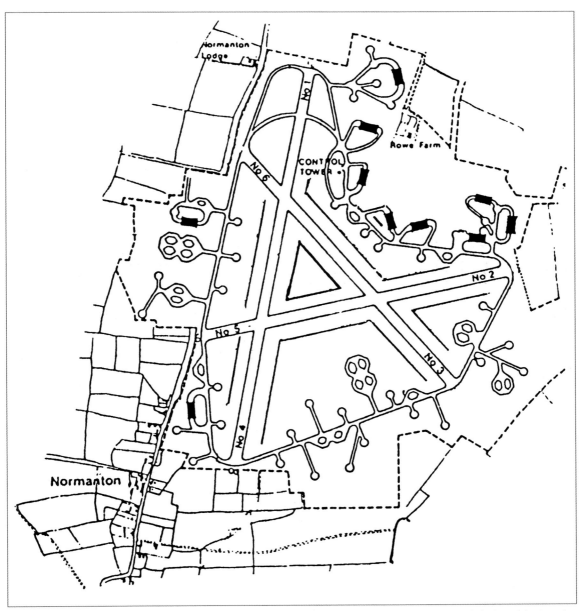

A plan of the hamlet of Normanton, 1944. It shows the extensive airfield that dominated the area during the Second World War. Bottesford airfield was constructed in the early years of the war, and opened on 10 September 1941. The commanding officer was Group Captain W.G. Cheshire. Bomber Command stationed Lancaster bombers on the airfield, and hundreds of attacking raids were made into occupied Europe from this very important base. The German air force made their first raid on the airfield in November 1940, during the construction of the runway. On 9 and 16 May 1941 the Luftwaffe bombed the Vale of Belvoir – possibly as many as ten high-explosive bombs fell in and around the airfield. The air was thick with German aircraft and machine-guns being fired upwards towards the incoming planes. The final raid on the airfield took place on 20 March 1945 when a lone Ju188 dropped Butterfly bombs on the airfield and machine-gunned one of the hangars.

BELVOIR CASTLE

This castle is situated in a dominant position on the hill overlooking the Vale of Belvoir into Nottinghamshire and Lincolnshire. It is an ideal site for a castle, controlling the major roads north and south. The Fosse Way to Newark and the Great North Road to Ermine Street, are east of the castle site. After the Norman Conquest William found it necessary to build temporary castles throughout his new kingdom. This natural site to the north-east on the edge of Leicestershire was ideal. On top of this hill in about 1080 Robert de Todeni, William's standard-bearer at the Battle of Hastings, was instructed to erect a motte. After his death in 1088 his son constructed a stone keep in the centre of the site, and used the surname Albini. William Albini was one of the barons who opposed King John in 1216. The king laid siege to the castle, taking it by storm and demolishing most of the protective defences. In 1267 Albini's daughter married Robert de Ros, who rebuilt the defensive walls and extended the keep on the instructions of Henry III. The Lancastrian Thomas, Lord Ros was executed by Edward IV. William, Lord Hastings, on being granted Ashby de la Zouch Castle, immediately attacked Belvoir Castle in 1464, storming the walls aftera very short siege and slaying many of the occupiers. Belvoir Castle was restored to the Ros family by Henry VII in 1485. The castle lay in ruins until the 1520s. The Ros family had no sons; the daughter of Lord Ros, Eleanor, married Sir Robert Manners, sheriff of Northumberland. Eleanor died in 1487. The castle stood in ruins and it was not until the reign of Henry VIII that the site was considered worth occupation again, when Sir Robert's grandson was created the 1st Earl of Rutland by the king. A mansion in the East Midlands was needed to justify the family's position in high society. Elizabeth I believed the 5th Earl of Rutland was implicated in the Essex rebellion against her, and he was imprisoned in the Tower of London, and only released from prison by James I. The Rutland family supported the Parliamentary cause in the Civil War. They had reservations about the position of the monarchy in the seventeenth century.

An extract from John Prior's map of
Leicestershire published in 1777. Belvoir
Castle is indicated on the top of a sharp,
round hill. To the left are the ruins of
St James's Church at Woolsthorpe.

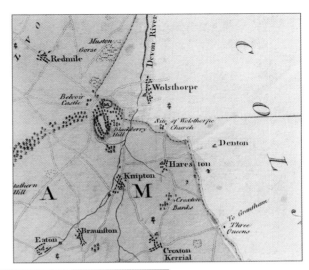

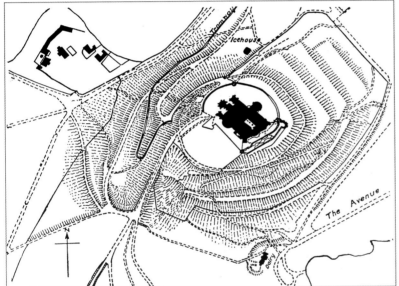

A plan of Blackberry Hill and
the site of Belvoir Castle,
published in 1907.

Opposite: Belvoir Castle, *c.* 1630. This engraving produced in the early nineteenth century is an interpretation
of how this castle stood on the hill overlooking the Vale of Belvoir. On 28 January 1643 the castle was lightly
garrisoned by a hundred Parliamentary troops and servants who owed loyalty to the 8th Earl of Rutland.
Gervase Lucas, the earl's master of horse, had left his service because of his loyalty to the king. Lucas was very
well acquainted with the layout of the castle. After dark, with eight men, Lucas crept up to the walls of the
castle and cast a rope around one of the decorative pinnacles. Lucas climbed into the castle and opened the
main gate. The troop of just over a hundred Royalist soldiers took the defenders completely by surprise, and
Lucas was granted a knighthood. Belvoir Castle became a nightmare for the Parliamentary troops in the area
because it was easily defended and impossible to capture by direct attack because of the volume of captured
cannon that were in situ. Parliament gave Lucas the title Commander-in-Chief of the Fen Robbers; he
launched raids from the castle throughout Leicestershire, Nottinghamshire and well into Lincolnshire, until
finally surrendering when all were lost for the king's cause.

The ruins of the church of St James on the road from Harston to Woolsthorpe, 1792. On the hill in the background stands the manor house being built on the site of Belvoir Castle incorporating some of the castle ruins. Cromwellian troops used this church as defensive barracks as it was in range of the cannon fired from the castle. Even though the castle was overlooked by Cromwellian troops, Charles I took refuge there on the evening of 3 November 1645, on his way south from Newark. He left the castle for Oxford next morning protected by a hundred mounted Cavaliers. Under siege Belvoir Castle was impossible to attack. All the trees and shrubs had been removed, and the escarpment around the castle was very steep from the south, east and west with a long rise from the north, with excellent lines for cannon fire. To attack the castle by approaching through sapping up the hill with trenches was out of the question.

The remains of St James's Church on the Harston road. After a lengthy siege Sir Gervase Lucas and all the king's soldiers were allowed to march out from Belvoir Castle to Lichfield on 3 February 1646. This surrender was negotiated with the help of the 8th Earl of Rutland who did not want his castle destroyed.

An artistic impression of Belvoir Castle mansion house, published in the 1740s. The escarpment is too steep. In 1703 Queen Anne raised the earldom of Rutland to a dukedom; possibly as a result of this, major landscaping of the hill to such a degree took place.

Considerable additions and changes took place to re-create a castle on Blackberry Hill. This engraving of Belvoir Castle, drawn by F.W.L. Stockdale, was published on 1 January 1815.

On the restoration of Charles II in 1660, it is presumed that the 8th Earl's loyalties switched. This photograph of Belvoir Castle was taken in 1905.

The Belvoir peacock on the defensive walls of the castle, May 2003. The peacock surmounts the Rutland coat of arms of the Manners family of Northumberland, Derbyshire and Leicestershire, Dukes of Rutland.

Jousting at Belvoir Castle, May 2003.

One of the forms of training for war on horseback during the medieval period was the tournament. This included jousting with shield and lance, charging on horseback and practising with the two-handed heavy sword. A step back in time is taken in this re-enactment of May 2003.

A Civil War re-enactment by the Siege Group, 27 May 2001. This scene shows Royalists suffering under an attack – but the Parliamentarians were never successful. The troops in the castle surrendered in 1646.

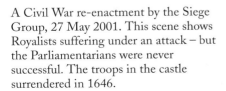

KING LUD'S ENTRENCHMENTS

The Romans had attempted to occupy Britain for some years before they partially succeeded, under Julius Caesar. The Bronze Age and Iron Age people who occupied Britain before the Roman occupation ran a highly civilised country, with laws and a system of government organised and controlled by various chiefs or kings. King Lud may have been one of these. He is thought to have been the builder of a wall around a town on the River Thames, eventually to be called London. Hence the name Ludgate, part of the city of London, with its walled entrance gate. During the late nineteenth century considerable historical and archaeological research was conducted by wealthy amateurs to record local history. Some of this research has doubtful origins; much is based on local gossip, handed down by generations through the family. Lud's entrenchments must fall into this category. They are indicated on the Ordnance Survey on the Saltby to Wyville road that crosses the Viking Way, the county boundary between Leicestershire and Lincolnshire.

The entrenchments are considered to be a defence system that stretches for about three-quarters of a mile in an area of open land between two heavily wooded forests. It would seem to be a ditch and rampart fortification to defend a kingdom against advancing armies. A number of Bronze Age barrows are located in the vicinity of the fortification. In 1978 one of the barrows was excavated in a controlled dig, indicated by 'A' below.

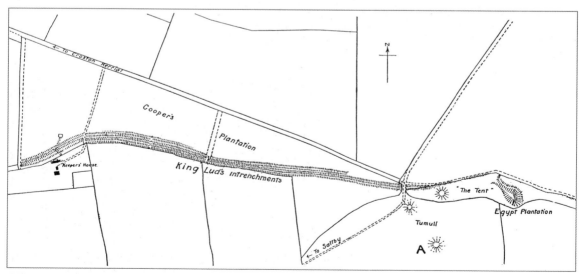

King Lud's entrenchments from a drawing of 1906, based on the Ordnance Survey. The ditch is still visible through the trees on the minor road, extending from the junction of the Saltby to Wyville road, leading to Croxton Kerrial. This accurate plan indicates the largest of the three tumuli (barrows) at A.

The remains of King Lud's entrenchment, March 2003. The embankment and ditch are clearly visible through the trees in Coopers Plantation. To view these earthworks it is necessary to visit the site during the winter and early spring. The site can be seen from the minor road to Croxton Kerrial, as indicated on the plan opposite.

Excavation of the Bronze Age barrow near King Lud's entrenchments, 1978. The burial site was constructed in about 1950 BC. Here the low circular wall, central to the layout, is in evidence. Just visible is the position of the primary burial, consisting of a cremation placed in a small wooden coffin.

A twentieth-century encampment in Cooper's Plantation on the junction with the Saltby to Croxton Kerrial road. During the Second World War Saltby airfield was built. It opened in August 1941. Cooper's Plantation and many acres of farmland were incorporated into the airfield. Outlying units were erected, some very close to King Lud's entrenchment. This ruin stands very close to the Bronze Age site of a prehistoric battlefield. History indeed repeats itself.

SALTBY AIRFIELD

Saltby airfield was constructed on Saltby Heath. German intelligence in the early years of the Second World War was excellent. The Luftwaffe were well aware that an aerodrome was being built in this remote part of Leicestershire on the Lincolnshire border. Work began on the site in 1940; woods, spinneys and heathland were destroyed, even the burial sites of long dead Bronze Age warriors were threatened and some destroyed. Rare flora and fauna were lost for ever.

On 9 January 1941 the first bombing raid occurred. A Luftwaffe dive bomber strafed the site, dropping three bombs, one of which accurately hit and demolished the Home Guard base on the heath. It is presumed that the Home Guard or troops guarding the site had opened fire. If so, the navigator on the attacking plane certainly was very well trained – or lucky. An extensive raid by German aircraft was made on the site in April 1941, dropping a number of bombs and damaging the main runway. A machine-gun battle developed.

After the war was over Luftwaffe photographic records were found of Saltby airfield, obviously taken by German reconnaissance aircraft.

The 1943 control tower which has now been demolished, seen in 1969. Fauna is returning to parts of the ancient heath.

These photographs were taken on 8 November 1940, and the layout of the site is clearly indicated. The final raids on the airfield took place on 13 and 20 August 1941, a few days before the site was officially opened. According to War Office records thirty bombs were dropped in or around Saltby airfield. Unexploded bombs are not recorded – how many still lie deep down in the farmland around this wartime airfield? One was certainly found near the runway and was dealt with by a bomb disposal unit. There is no record of any deaths, though a number of personnel were wounded.

Saltby is recorded as one of the major airfields used for conveying towed gliders with airborne troops to Normandy on 5 June 1944. On 17 September 1944 gliders from Saltby conveyed the 2nd, 3rd, 11th and 156th Battalions of the British 1st Parachute Brigade to Arnhem. From this site two days later the 1st Polish Parachute Brigade was sent to Arnhem, and their place in history.

The wartime airfield is not dead; in about 1971 the Buckminster Gliding Club took up residence on part of the extensive site, and uses one of the main runways.

A plan of Saltby airfield, a satellite of Cottesmore in Rutland. It was equipped with Hampden, Anson and Wellington bombers, to be used in air raids on occupied Europe. In February 1944 the American air force took over the airfield and it became USAAF Station 538. Today it is the home of Buckminster Gliding Club. Compare this plan with the photographs below.

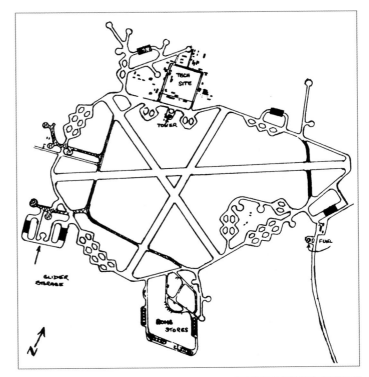

The main runway at Saltby airfield taken by the author from the aircraft Robin, G-7064, 4 September 2003.

Ready for take-off. Mary Jones and Margaret Williams in a Blanik glider, with Pam Hickman in the background, at Saltby airfield, July 1985.

David Epton in the Robin, waiting for the author to board before viewing this historic Second World War airfield from the air, on Thursday 4 September 2003.

SEWSTERN LANE

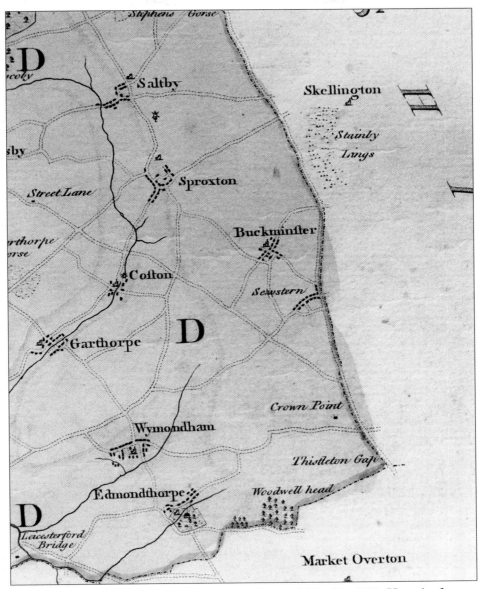

An extract from John Prior's map of Leicestershire, published in 1777. Here the famous Sewstern Lane is indicated from Thistleton Gap to Stephens Gorse, a roadway that forms the border of Leicestershire with Lincolnshire. Today it is part of the Viking Way, a long-distance footpath. In the Middle Ages it was a very important highway and during the English Civil War it was a roadway that carried much ordnance and many troops, after the nearby Great North Road became impassable. Stainby Lings is indicated on this map, the site on Sewstern Lane of a skirmish that took place in the Civil War.

Plukney Dale on Sewstern Lane, overgrown with bushes and trees, June 2003. This is still an ideal site for an ambush. On John Prior's map of 1777 this area is indicated as scrubland.

Opposite, top: The Red Lion public house at Sewstern, 1916. This was the site of a most macabre incident that took place in the Civil War. A record of the minor battle that happened on Sewstern Lane is now part of local folklore. Conflicting accounts have been published; the version that was perpetuated in the bar at the Red Lion and handed down by word of mouth for generations is a reasonably accurate account.

Belvoir Castle was a Royalist stronghold and to the south Burley-on-the-Hill in Rutland was held by Parliamentarian forces. Many raiding parties were organised by the Commander-in-Chief of the Fen Robbers into Lincolnshire from Belvoir Castle. Colonel Gervase Lucas organised a raid into Lincolnshire and Rutland to steal cattle on Christmas Eve 1643 when he considered the Parliamentarians would be celebrating at Burley-on-the-Hill. Lieutenant-Captain Allen, the Parliamentarian governor, was warned of the Fen Robbers' raid. He laid an ambush on Sewstern Lane at Stainby Lings in a natural hollow surrounded by conifers. Captain Plukney, a Royalist from Belvoir, was killed. The victorious Roundheads under the leadership of Allen, the captain of horse from Burley-on-the-Hill, threw Plukney's body across his horse, and proceeded to the Red Lion to celebrate the victory. The horse was tethered in the paddock at the rear of the inn with the captured cattle while the Roundheads refreshed themselves with the strong local ale. Venturing out of the inn on the way back to Burley-on-the-Hill they encountered an avenging troop of horse from Belvoir Castle and Allen was killed. His troopers fled. The Royalists then proceeded to the Red Lion with Allen's body thrown across his horse. It was tethered alongside Plukney's. According to a villager named Thorpe neither of the two was quite dead, even though they had both been run through with swords, and they rolled their eyes at each other in agony until they passed away.

The Red Lion, now a private house situated off the Stamford Road on Sewstern Lane. At the rear is a vegetable garden, formerly the paddock where the cattle and horses were kept during the Civil War incident of 1643.

PAIN'S SIDINGS

During the First World War people were frightened by the prospect of Zeppelins flying over England unopposed, and dropping bombs with little resistance. As the war progressed this did change. The Zeppelin was one type of airship, but there were others. The national press classed all German airships that bombed targets in England as Zeppelins. The most successful was the military airship designed by Graf von Zeppelin. Johann Schütte designed a reasonably successful airship, the Schütte-Lanz, that also operated over England during the First World War. These very slow airships flew at a height that was too high for aeroplanes to reach. They had been developed by the German war machine between 1914 and 1916. Slow flights of military airships flew across the North Sea attacking towns and cities with ease. The object was to bomb at night, seeking a direction on the ground by following railway lines across the countryside. Many such flights took place across Leicestershire. Loughborough was subjected to a bombing raid by a German airship in January 1916, when a number of people were killed. Defences were constructed with the use of searchlight batteries at selected sites considered to be of military importance and on the line of military airship flight paths.

On 2 September 1916 a flight of three military airships left Trier in Germany. Made up of two Zeppelins, L790 and L798, and a Schütte-Lanz airship, SLXI, captained by Hauptmann Schramm. The target was London where L790 and L798 dropped their bombs. The Schütte-Lanz was unsuccessful because of low cloud and decided to follow the railway line north out of the city of London. This daytime flight appeared very frightening to the watchers below. Orders must have been given to bomb industrial sites, for when this airship arrived over Nottingham it bombed the Stanton Ironworks on the afternoon of 2 September. On leaving Nottingham SLXI followed the railway lines east, possibly being helped by a train conveying mineral wagons to the iron-ore mines near Melton Mowbray. This would be on the flight back to Germany, and Schramm could use the system of railway tracks to reach the south-east coast. Now the countryside would be awake, defences would be informed. The small searchlight battery near Thistleton Gap on the Leicestershire, Lincolnshire and Rutland border, was made aware that 'the Zep was coming' along the railway to Pain's Sidings.

Artist's impression of the German imperial army airship, exposed by a pair of searchlights, 1916.

The Saxby to Bourne railway line was opened on 5 June 1893 principally to carry goods, and in north-east Leicestershire to convey iron-ore wagons to Stanton Ironworks. James Pain laid out and built Pain's Sidings to serve the recently opened-up Market Overton open-cast iron-ore mines in 1907. The military airship passed over the north of the village of Wymondham. It was noisy enough for the whole village to be aware of it passing overhead. The small group of local volunteers of the Royal Defence Corps were notified by telephone that the airship was coming their way. This lightly armed group was in charge of a pair of searchlights, and positioned at the railway sidings that controlled the conveyance of iron ore to be used in the manufacture of munitions. Was this an accidental attack, or was there advance planning by the German war machine? The lights were switched on, illuminating the airship. It dropped six to eight bombs. Dick Beecroft ordered the group to open fire, the crew in the airship fired back. Bombs were scattered across the railway lines and into the iron-ore workings. No injuries were sustained on the ground and only a small amount of damage was caused. One of the bomb handles was retrieved; it is now on display in Wymondham Village Hall.

Still following the railway lines the Schütte-Lanz airship followed the east coast railway line towards London. The Royal Flying Corps, 39 Squadron, were well aware that a German military airship was travelling south. Well prepared, Lieutenant William Leefe Robinson managed to fly his aeroplane high enough to get under the airship which had lost height. He opened fire with his machine-guns which were armed with incendiary ammunition and scored direct hits. Schütte-Lanz airframes were made of wood, and as the airship burst into flames, it collapsed around Lieutenant Robinson; he was lucky to escape with his life. The bullets from Dick Beecroft's group had pierced the envelope of the airship, so causing it to lose gas and height. Robinson was awarded the Victoria Cross for this action. He survived the First World War, but died in the influenza epidemic on 31 December 1918 aged twenty-three.

The Schütte-Lanz crashed into a field at Cuffley in Hertfordshire. A memorial obelisk has been erected near the site. This was the beginning of the end of airship attacks on England. Improvements to British aircraft enabled them to fly higher, so they could hit back at the raiding German airships.

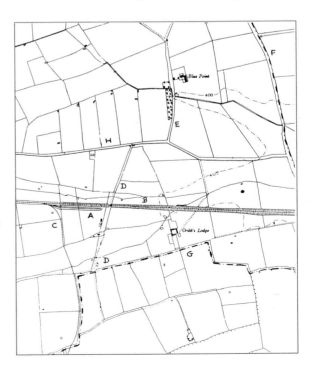

An extract from an estate plan based on the Ordnance Survey, published in 1920.

A. Pain's Sidings
B. The Saxby–Bourne railway line
C. Mineral railway line to Market Overton quarries
D. Public footpath
E. The Viking Way
F. The Lincolnshire–Leicestershire border
G. The Rutland–Leicestershire border
H. Wymondham Drift.

The remains of a handle from one of the bombs dropped on Pain's Sidings. This is now attached to the south-facing wall inside Wymondham Village Hall.

A Schütte-Lanz airship in the hangar at Rheinau, 1916.

Inside the control gondola of a Schütte-Lanz airship of the type that bombed Pain's Sidings in the early morning of 3 September 1916.

Blue-brick remains of the base of the nineteenth-century railway bridge built to carry the Saxby–Bourne railway line.
In the copse that is visible to the right of this photograph is the site of Pain's Sidings.
In one of these fields the searchlights were erected. This is where local troops attacked the German airship.

Left: Hauptmann Wilhelm Schramm of the German Army Airship Division, the commander of the airship SLXI, in which he was killed at Cuffley on 3 September 1916. *Right:* Lieutenant William Leefe Robinson VC, 1916. 'He attacked an enemy airship under circumstances of great difficulty and danger and sent it crashing to the ground as a flaming wreck.'

Part of the remains of the Schütte-Lanz airship, lying in a field at Cuffley, 3 September 1916.

BATTLE OF SAXBY

This was hardly a battle in the strict sense of the word. Certainly no individual was killed. It was a battle, nonetheless, between two opposing sides in a vicious conflict, brought about by two wealthy individuals, George Hudson and Robert, 6th Earl of Harborough. George Hudson, the 'Railway King', was chairman of the Midland Counties Railway. By the 1840s he was a very rich man. This railway company was formed in the 1830s by a group of moneyed coalmine owners. The railway system expanded throughout the Midlands, through cash investments, involving influential shareholders and well supported in the House of Lords. As part of the expansion programme to move coal across the country, in 1844 interest was generated to construct a railway from Syston to Peterborough, which would connect the east coast railway with the Midlands system. It would enable coal excavated at the expanding deep coal mines at Whitwick and Snibston to link into the national railway system.

The line of this new railway would pass through Melton Mowbray, Stapleford Park, Oakham, Stamford and on to Peterborough. The effect of opening this railway on the Melton to Oakham canal would be catastrophic. This small canal system, 15½ miles long, opened in December 1802. It contained eighteen locks and there was never much return to its shareholders. Landowners and adjacent farmers used the system to convey large quantities of goods on the barges to and from the urban areas that had opened up in the countryside. They would have gained considerable benefit from this canal. Agricultural products were the main source of income from the area. Inward, of course, were coal and house-building materials. The new railway would take away all of the coal trade from the canal. The shareholders were principally coalmine owners. One of the main landowners was Lord Harborough. Robert, the

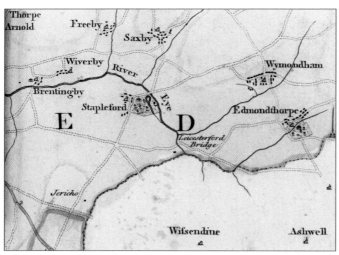

Prior's map of 1777 indicating Lord Harborough's park.

4th Earl, supported the construction of the canal across the north of the enclosed park at Stapleford. During the construction of the canal he was not as generous as he could have been, and restricted the use of the water from the river and streams flowing through his land. The deviation of the canal to the north of his home also ensured that four extra locks had to be constructed and an expensive four-arched culvert built at Saxby across the Garthorpe Brook. On the death of the 4th Earl in 1799, the nominated trustees acted on behalf of the estate, for Philip, 5th Earl of Harborough, who died eight years later in 1807. Robert, his son, the 6th Earl, took on the role of lord of the manor, under the direction of the trustees, covering many of the villages centred on Stapleford Hall. On reaching maturity in 1818 he retained the Harborough shares in the Melton to Oakham canal. On examining the minute books of the Oakham Canal Company and reading the records of the meetings held between May 1831 and February 1843 there are forty references to claims and counterclaims involving the 6th Earl of Harborough. It is presumed after gaining complete control of the numerous estates after they were released by the executive trustees that he proceeded to run his affairs from his enclosed park at Stapleford. He had inherited a considerable income of £20,000 to £30,000 per annum and a lump sum of £125,000, a vast amount in the early part of the nineteenth century. With such quantities of ready cash he developed a cavalier attitude with a very unsociable behaviour to all and sundry. He rebuilt the deer fence, refusing to allow the two local hunts, the Belvoir and Cottesmore, to enter the park, even proceeding to the extent of lining the fox coverts with dog spears. It is obvious that this pugnacious nobleman was only interested in his own domain. He built a beautiful cottage near the lake, where he lived with his mistress Emma Sarah Love. She had five children by Harborough of whom two sons survived. But these children were bastards and could not inherit the title or estate. On 27 November 1843 the 6th Earl married Mary Eliza Temple. They had no children. The 6th Earl was a mixed-up individual who felt life was against him.

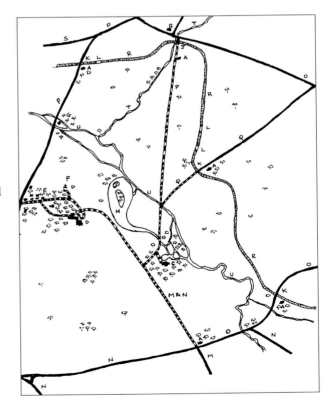

Site of the Battle of Saxby

A   Gamekeeper's cottages
B   Possible site of the public house
C   Lord Harborough's cottage
D   Stapleford Hall
C   St Mary Magdalene's Church
D   Market Cross
E   Cottages
F   Site of the 'cleared' village of Stapleford
G   Watermill
H   Lake
J   Bridge
K   Swing bridge
L   Locks
M   Hollygate Farm Road
N   Whissendine Road
O   Wymondham Road
P   Saxby Road
Q   The Strete
R   The Melton to Oakham canal
S   Melton Road
T   Garthorpe Brook
U   River Eye

In 1833 he closed the public house, the Harborough Arms, which stood close to the Melton to Oakham canal at Saxby. This deprived canal workers, local villagers and his own employees from using the facilities that were on offer at this inn. During the 1830s, if his legal actions had been successful, he would have bankrupted the Oakham Canal Company, as it was he who made the use of the canal along the north side of his park as unpleasant as possible. He obtained an Act of Parliament against private individuals. They were trespassing on the tow-path along the side of the canal that passed through his estate; only canal users could travel along the canal, walking with the moving barges. On p. 157 there is an extract from the Ordnance Survey, published in 1835 and revised in 1867, which clearly indicates six lodges that housed gamekeepers. These cottages were erected to prevent entrance to Stapleford Park from the public highway at all road junctions and bridges. These gamekeepers also acted as gatekeepers, opening and closing the swing bridges across the canal. There were four bridges that crossed the canal into Lord Harborough's park, three of which were swing bridges, in the 1840s.

In 1843 Lord Harborough's attitude towards the Oakham Canal Company changed completely. This pugnacious lord was opposed to the installation of a railway system to convey coal across land owned by him. He published a notice: 'Surveyors will not be permitted to enter upon his Lordship's land.' On 23 October 1844 a meeting was arranged in Oakham where George Hudson, Robert Stephenson and John Ellis represented the Midland Railway Company, with their solicitor Mr Macauley. Representing the Oakham Canal Company and Lord Harborough was William Latham, the Melton Mowbray solicitor. Latham addressed the meeting stating that building a railway line across the land would sustain injuries to Harborough's land and properties. He and the Oakham Canal Company would oppose the railway; Harborough would provide the money necessary to oppose the scheme. On 15 November 1844 a meeting was called in Loughborough on behalf of the Melton Navigation by their solicitor William Latham. Representatives of the Oakham Canal Company were in attendance. Under discussion was the likely effect of the Syston–Peterborough railway line being built and operated. It was apparent that the sale of the Oakham Canal Company to the Midland Railway Company was the only sound decision to make, but Harborough was still determined to oppose the building of the railway, with the aid of considerable cash and some of his friends in the House of Lords. Undoubtedly George Hudson was also aware of the financial support he would eventually obtain from his supporters in the House of Lords, especially because the shares issued on the Midland Railway Company were proving to be an excellent investment. Returns on shares in the Oakham Canal Company were very poor. An offer of £26,000 was made by the Midland Railway Company to purchase the Melton to Oakham canal. He was certain that he would build this railway, so Hudson instructed his surveyors to commence measuring the route of the railway line, even though no final agreement between the two parties had been obtained. Hudson must have known that many of the shareholders of the unprofitable canal would sell, especially on the terms on offer. The Melton to Oakham canal cost £68,120 to build. It never made any profit for the first ten years and was a very poor investment until it was closed.

One of Lord Harborough's gamekeeper's cottages. This historic cottage still stands on the edge of Stapleford Park on the Wymondham to Stapleford road. The canal passed very close to this cottage, and it is to the north-east of this cottage that the railway workers and their supporters entered the park to commence battle on 16 November 1844.

On Tuesday 12 November 1844 battle commenced. This was well planned by both sides of the conflict, and solicitors for both parties were present. Railway surveyors walked along the tow-path into the park to start measuring out the line of the projected railway. Gamekeeper Todd, on the instruction of Lord Harborough, told the surveyors to stop; one pulled out a pistol, pointing it at Todd, who shouted 'Shoot away'. A group of gamekeepers and farmworkers charged the surveyors, nine of whom were captured, and put in 'a muck cart' to be conveyed to John Turner JP at Cold Overton Hall, 6 miles away, to be charged with trespass. The JP was away from his home, so the surveyors were released by tipping the muck cart and depositing the nine prisoners covered in manure, on to the highway. A few days later various cross-summonses were issued at the Melton Mowbray Police Court. Two days later the railway team returned, backed by a strong body of navvies and at least three prize-fighters from Nottingham, along with a number of surveyors and a solicitor named Hough who was organising the railway contingent. William Latham and Lord Harborough's steward, Fabling, were in charge of the Stapleford squad, made up of an assortment of gamekeepers, canal lock-keepers and farm workers, about forty people in all. The scene was set at Saxby Bridge at 9 a.m. The railworkers, led by Hough, marched along the banks of the canal from Melton Mowbray. The opposition had erected a barricade of drays and a staked fence at the bridge.

The railway workers charged the prepared defences with no luck. Both sides were in the process of calling up reinforcements when five county policemen turned up and threatened to arrest the first person who recommenced the fracas. Both sides were ordered to lay down their arms. On advice from the police (one wonders why?) they were ordered to enter into a competition by forming two living barriers, and pushing against each other. By this time many individuals from the surrounding villages had turned up to view the spectacle. Through the heaving and shoving involving some eighty people it must have had the appearance of a large rugby scrum. How many workers fell into the canal is not known. Utterly exhausted, many of the participants climbed over each other to avoid being crushed. Through fatigue, the two walls of people collapsed, covered in mud and slime from the surrounding ditches and the canal. Possibly this is what the police officers wanted. Some railway workers away from the fracas managed to lay out a chain on the tow-path and commence a series of measurements; seen by some advancing gamekeepers they were beaten up and the chain broken. William Latham called a truce, suggesting that matters should be resolved at various police court actions to be held in Melton Mowbray on 19 November.

Threats of court action did not deter the Midland Railway Company from surveying the line of this projected railway. William Latham published the notice that Lord Harborough would defend his barricades with cannon from his yacht. At 7 a.m. on 16 November a small party of railway workers began measuring the tow-path in Freeby parish, part of Lord Harborough's estate. These surveyors were very easily repelled by a large force of Harborough's men, who confiscated the chains and destroyed them. This was a ruse by the railway; while this small fight was taking place over 100 men were entering the park near Saxby Bridge, climbing over the deer fence palings off the Wymondham road. They began measuring the land until they came opposite the cottage in the trees near the lake. Lord Harborough was enraged and ordered Fabling to attack the intruders and destroy the measuring chains. They fought back; Harborough's men retreated. Brown, the lock-keeper who possibly lived in the lodge opposite the cottage, rendered great assistance. A powerful man with sound fists, he sent railway workers head over heels with every blow. Harborough's men eventually held their ground by building a barricade of wagons and hurdles. Fabling brought up a fire engine to pump water over the railway workers. Events took a serious turn when the surveyors and railwaymen took up their measuring poles as lances and charged the defensive position. Many of Harborough's men received serious wounds, and it was a miracle that no one was killed. A sharp pointed lance piercing a chest wall could have been fatal. The railwaymen eventually lost heart and retreated when Lord Harborough arrived with two cannon, which he had removed from his yacht on the lake and strapped on to a cart. How powerful these cannon were is not known, but the sight of them was enough to make the surveyors and navvies run for their lives. The railway army was well organised; they all had white ribbons in their buttonholes to distinguish them from Harborough's troops. Fabling, on behalf of his employer, paid his men a bonus of 2s 6d per day.

Undoubtedly some planning had taken place with regard to these fights. This must have been obvious to the county police. The first court cases were held on

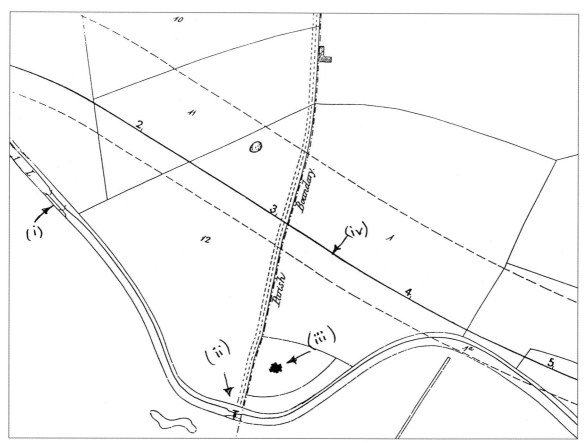

This is part of the plan from the *Book of Reference*, circulated in November 1846, detailing the deviations of the railway line to the north of Lord Harborough's cottage in Stapleford park. (i) This indicates lock number twelve. (ii) Indicates the swing bridge on The Strete, the Roman road connecting the highway to the north of Wymondham. (iii) Gamekeeper's cottage, built before the Oakham canal was laid out and completed in this area in the summer of 1801. This gamekeeper's cottage was erected to control entry into Stapleford Park from the public highway. Possibly the gamekeeper was also a lock-keeper and would certainly have opened and closed the swing bridge, preventing unwanted people entering the park. The canal was acting as a medieval moat. (iv) The projected line of the Syston–Peterborough railway line. It is interesting to note that the 4th Earl of Harborough, when agreeing to the line that the Oakham canal should take, insisted that a bend in the canal should be constructed south of one of the lodges, indicated on this plan, that obviously controlled the highway into the park.

19 November 1844. John Todd, Lord Harborough's senior gamekeeper, was charged with assault on 12 November. Thomas Hibbons of Oakham and nine others were charged with assault on 16 November. Evidence was given that Lord Harborough was present at the battle on 16 November with two small cannon and had to be restrained from opening fire. It was suggested that they were cannon for starting yacht races; even so, if they had been loaded with lead shot from close range, and if any of those receiving the charge had been hit,

some of the attacking force could have been killed. This case was committed to the Leicester Assizes and was held on 26 March 1845.

At the Assizes Chief Justice Tindal found the ten Midland railway workers guilty of assault, fined them 1s each and sentenced them all to one month in jail. In the chief justice's opinion they were all guilty of causing a riot and Lord Harborough had every right to resist their entrance to his park and was justified in using force to eject them. Mr Ward, a railway worker, was awarded £8 for Lord Harborough's men damaging a theodolite. Lord Harborough's solicitor presented a counterclaim against Ward for trespass on 16 November; Ward and Cope were sentenced to one month in jail.

On 19 April 1845 the Oakham Canal Company on a majority decision decided to sell the canal and all its fittings to the Midland Railway Company. This did not dissuade Lord Harborough from continuing his opposition to the railway company. On 24 November 1845 surveyors with railway employees were attempting to measure the railway deviation to the north of Stapleford Park. This party consisted of more than 150 people. Harborough arrived in a gig with sheets of calico supported on sets of wooden rails, similar to the sails on his yacht. He drove his gig up and down the highway to prevent the surveyors from laying out the site with their theodolites. The surveyors were in uproar, but they still continued to lay out the line. A large group of gamekeepers arrived on the scene, so changing the course of the conflict. Harborough instructed one of his farmworkers to drive a brake against one of the surveyors, with Charles Liddall in his chaise, forcing it into the ditch. He then ordered his employees to saw the wheels off the chaise. That stopped work for the day. On 28 November action took place on the highway once again. Harborough was incensed by Mr Adam, who had acted for the Oakham Canal Company as a legal representative in the previous court actions. He had 'turned his coat' and now was acting as a legal representative on behalf of the Midland Railway Company. Harborough and Adam stood toe to toe in a bare-fist fight on the highway. It was declared a draw and both sides withdrew, the matter to be resolved in the court of law. The court case in question was held at Nottingham Assizes on 24 July 1846. The case was the Midland Railway Company v Lord Harborough and twelve unknown persons for their action to prevent Charles Liddall and others from taking surveys and planning the route of the projected railway to be laid before Parliament and for assaulting Charles Liddell and others. The jury retired, and after five hours' deliberation they returned and delivered a verdict of 'Not guilty' on all charges against Lord Harborough. The Midland Railway Company purchased the Oakham Canal Company for the final sum of approximately £34,000 plus a quantity of shares. It became law on 27 July 1846, three days after the court case at Nottingham Assizes.

Lord Harborough won a partial victory over the Midland Railway Company. To avoid Stapleford Park the railway company obtained an Act of Parliament on 2 June 1846 to construct a tunnel under Cuckoo Plantation, with the railway passing through farmland at Stapleford owned by Lord Harborough. The tunnel was too shallow and collapsed, uprooting sixty trees. Harborough brought out an immediate injunction. The terms of the Act were quite clear: no trees must be damaged. As a result of this a further Act of Parliament was needed to make a deviation to the recommended line of the railway. This ended in the famous 'Lord Harborough's curve' between Stapleford and Saxby and resulted in the building of a wooden bridge across the Garthorpe Brook, to be known as Pile Bridge.

On 1 May 1848 the first through trains left Leicester at 6 a.m. and Peterborough at 5.35 a.m., arriving at the same time at Oakham. Unfortunately the purchase of the Oakham Canal Company by the Midland Railway Company had only one object in mind: to close the canal, and sell off all of the surplus land and buildings. The locks were demolished, and gates, bricks and other materials were offered at various auctions on site.

The Harborough coat of arms.

Lord Harborough's cottage, standing in the trees east of Stapleford Hall in the park, south of the lake, 1832. The cottage was built by Robert, 6th Earl of Harborough. He disliked the hall, possibly because he could not entertain his mistress there, the Drury Lane actress Emma Sarah Love. She lived with him for twenty-five years and gave birth to five children. The two who survived retained the Harborough family name of Sherard. Harborough laid out an extensive water garden in front of this cottage, clearly indicated in the drawing above. This pugnacious earl was incensed when the Midland Railway Company wished to build a railway across his land in easy view of this cottage.

All that remains of the impressive cottage that stood in the trees near Stapleford Hall. This wood is now marked on the Ordnance Survey as the Cottage Plantation. The cottage was demolished after the death of Lord Harborough in 1859 and a smaller version was rebuilt on the Stapleford Road in Whissendine, using much of the existing stone. Lady Harborough died in 1886. Before her death it is presumed that the cottage was given to Sarah Love, the 6th Earl's mistress.

The milepost which stands on the banks of the derelict canal, in a field off the Wymondham road, 1967. It is 5 miles from Melton Mowbray and 10½ from Oakham. It was very close to this canal milepost that most of the Battles of Saxby took place.

An aerial view of the site of Saxby Bridge, 1979. Compare this photograph with the one at the top of p. 156. There is a cherry tree next to the junction with the highway and the field track. This photograph was taken after heavy rain; the road leading to Saxby Bridge is clearly defined across the ridge and furrow.

The Oakham canal at Saxby, 1967. In the background stands the remnants of Pile Bridge on Lord Harborough's curve. One of the remaining piles is just visible on the base of the embankment to the left.

On 16 November 1844 the railway workers climbed the deer fence that Lord Harborough had erected around his park. In living memory this fence was virtually complete, being maintained by other owners of the estate. This photograph taken in 2003 is of the Harborough deer fence, which will never be repaired and is possibly a unique part of an historic battle.

The site of Saxby Bridge from Lord Harborough's curve looking north into the village of Saxby, 1967. The existing farm track is on the left; on the right is the remains of the highway into Stapleford Park. Saxby Bridge would have stood in the hedge indicated by the cherry tree that stands behind a slight mound next to the farm track.

This is the site of Saxby Bridge, early spring 2003. The photographer is standing on the road bridge over the Garthorpe Brook that runs into Stapleford Park. Compare this view with the aerial view on p. 154. On the left the highway leads to Wymondham.

The remains of the four-arched culverts that carried the Melton Mowbray to Oakham canal over Garthorpe Brook, through Stapleford Park, to connect with the River Eye, 2003. It is presumed that Saxby Bridge was built across the canal near this culvert. This again is the site of one of the vicious Battles of Saxby.

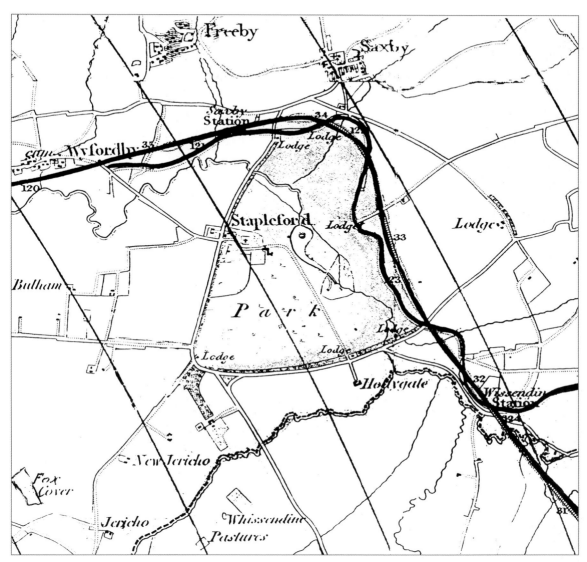

A section of the 1835 edition of the Ordnance Survey map, revised in 1867. On this map Stapleford Park is clearly defined; the Melton to Oakham canal and the Syston–Peterborough railway track are intertwined. When the map was first engraved in 1835 the railway did not exist. All the 'battles' of Saxby took place between Wyfordby and what is featured on this plan as Whissendine station. Six lodges used as gamekeepers' cottages are clearly indicated. Other estate workers would have lived in the small village of Stapleford. The Harborough cottage in the trees is indicated at the end of an approach road, near the lake. Cuckoo Hill Plantation is seen to the left of New Jericho, a fox cover. In the photograph on p. 158 the depression indicated in the centre running towards the plantation shows where the unsuccessful tunnel collapsed.

Cuckoo Hill Plantation, 1983.

Saxby railway station in 1930; it was built over the Melton to Oakham canal in 1849.

When the Syston–Peterborough railway line was completed bridges were built as soon as possible. To control the highway hand-operated crossing gates protecting the railway were built. On the Wymondham to Stapleford road a simple crossing was erected, with a gatekeeper's cottage. In 2003 this minor road is still controlled in exactly the same way as was the case in the second half of the nineteenth century.

THE BELER CONFLICT

It was in the valley along the River Wreake on a footpath between Rearsby and Brooksby that on 29 January 1326 a minor battle took place. It was one of the ongoing baronial wars, between a gathering of local adversaries. One protagonist was Sir Roger de Beler of nearby Kirby; after his death it was renamed Kirby Bellars. His main opponents were Sir Eustace de Folville, Lord of Ashby Folville, Sir Roger la Zouch of Ashby de la Zouch and Robert de Helewell. The result of this conflict was when Sir Roger de Beler joined King Edward II in support of the suppression of a group of Midland barons, not least Thomas of Lancaster, Earl of Leicester. Sir Roger de Beler, Sir Eustace la Zouch, and Robert de Helewell were part of the group of barons who opposed the king. Sir Roger changed sides, and was granted a pardon and considerable holdings in Leicestershire and the surrounding counties. He was appointed as magistrate of the Framland Hundred and summoned to attend the King's Council at London which ordered the execution of the Earl of Leicester. For one year, 1322, Sir Roger controlled the hundred from Leicester Castle.

He was a member of the noble family of de Mowbray, Dukes of Norfolk and lord of the manor of the nearby town, Melton Mowbray. These were welcomed to the court of the king. One of the local favourites of the king was the de Spensers, who owned property and the manor house at Loughborough. In nearby Ashby and at Lubbesthorpe lived the brothers, Roger and Ralph la Zouch. These two barons totally opposed the de Spensers. In 1322 they attacked a manor and farmland in a

The footpath between Brooksby and Rearsby, June 2003. This is the obvious site of the Beler battle of 1326.

controlled raid, removing so-called spoils of war. This property was owned by Hugh le Despencer, Earl of Winchester, a favourite of the king. The king appointed Sir Roger de Beler as commissioner to arrest the two main offending barons and bring them to trial on 28 May 1322. It is not known whether this was successful. The la Zouch family became Sir Roger's vicious enemy and joined forces with Sir Eustace de Folville, a local baron who had annoyed the king on unlawful action against his neighbours, not least Sir Roger de Beler. Sir Roger la Zouch, Ralph la Zouch and Sir Eustace de Folville, with his brothers, Walter and Robert de Helewell, recruited a small army to attack Sir Roger de Beler, the commissioner to the king on one of his journeys around the county as the lawful judge at the various assize courts. During these unsettled years when anarchy ruled again, after the death of Edward I, all court commissioners recruited armed soldiers to protect them when travelling to the appointed law courts.

Sir Roger la Zouch would have been well aware of the date and location of any assize courts. In January 1326 he planned to attack Sir Roger de Beler's armed group as they travelled towards Leicester where Sir Roger was to hold court. Sir Roger's retainers were well armed, with swords, spears and longbows. They were travelling along the valley on the south side of the River Wreake. Today this route is marked on the Ordnance Survey as a footpath stretching

Outside the church of St Michael, 2003. This footpath leads to Rearsby.

from Rearsby to Kirby Bellars and on to Melton Mowbray, where it joins the A607. Sir Roger la Zouch laid an ambush with his well-armed supporters, possibly hiding in scrubland and willow trees along the banks of the Wreake near Brooksby. A particularly vicious battle took place. The parties were well matched, and arrows flew, spears were smashed. How many soldiers recruited by both the group leaders were also killed or died of their wounds is not recorded, though it is on record that Sir Eustace de Folville killed Sir Roger de Beler with his sword. The small army that had attempted to defend the commissioner of the law retreated. To defend their retreat they fired a volley of arrows from their longbows. Sir Eustace de Folville, who led the charge, was struck down by an arrow entering his chest. He died from this wound three days later.

Sir Roger de Beler was buried in the church of St Peter at Kirby. Sir Eustace de Folville was buried in the church of St Mary at Ashby Folville. Alicia, the widow of Sir Roger de Beler, appealed to the king on a charge of murder against those who organised the ambush of her husband. In the year 1326 the whole country was in turmoil. Edward II had lost the Battle of Bannockburn in Scotland to Robert the Bruce, when most of the English army was killed along with many of his loyal barons. A leading baron, Roger Mortimer, invaded England with the king's estranged wife, Isabella. The baronial wars were at their height and minor battles took place throughout the country. After one such skirmish Mortimer captured the king on 16 November 1326. In January 1327 a committee of barons appointed Edward's son as king; there was considerable opposition to this, so secretly Mortimer gave instructions that Edward II must be killed, and this murder took place in Berkeley Castle on 21 September 1327. No wounds were to be visible on the body, so Edward was disembowelled by inserting red hot irons into the rectum.

With Edward II a prisoner, his son, nominally appointed King Edward III, empowered Henry de Lancaster, Earl of Leicester, the son of Thomas of Lancaster, who his father Edward II had executed, to take charge of the court of inquiry. On 28 February 1327 Edward III, at the age of fifteen, journeyed to Leicester where he stayed in the castle. The Earl of Leicester appointed three commissioners to hold the inquiry. The senior commissioner was Sir John Hamelin, knight of the shire, lord of the manor of Wymondham; he was given instructions to arrest Ralph la Zouch, Roger la Zouch, Walter de Folville, Robert de Folville, Adam de Bailey, William de Barkeston, Simon Hauberk, Robert de Helewell and Richard Folville, parson of the church of Teigh in Rutland. All of this motley crew were indicted of murder and had reportedly taken part in the ambush of the commissioner Roger de Beler. They all escaped, and were declared outlaws. Sir John Hamelin was given instructions to hunt them down throughout the counties involved, but he did not have much luck. In August 1327 they raided Sir John Hamelin's estate in Wymondham. They were repelled, but managed to steal nine sheep and load up a number of carts, stealing a considerable amount of grain and equipment. It would seem that Sir John Hamelin was not above acting illegally. Records exist that as a county baron he had raided the manor of Market Overton. On 10 March 1329 Edward III granted a general pardon to all who were involved. Sir Richard Folville was not included; it appears that he had been involved in one of the minor skirmishes against Roger Mortimer, who had appointed Edward III as king.

KIRBY BELLARS

An effigy of Roger de Beler in an engraving published in 1790. Sir Roger was killed in the battle near Rearsby in 1326, and buried in the church of St Peter. Roger de Beler obtained the manor of Kirby in 1319 from Roger de Zouch of Ashby de la Zouch. There was considerable bad feeling between these two knights of the shire. Possibly the Kirby estates were granted to Roger de Beler as a result of his support for the king in the baronial wars against Thomas of Lancaster, Earl of Leicester. Roger de Beler was an autocratic lord of the manor and commissioner to the county of Leicestershire, with the right to convict and execute all wrongdoers from this shire county. How many individuals from the lower class of the peasant community did he hang for minor offences, such as poaching and rustling cattle? This he did, and became a most unpopular county judge, disliked by all his neighbours, especially Sir Eustace de Folville. This was not helped by the fact that he was a friend of Edward II, who had appointed him as Baron of the Exchequer, possibly when Sir Roger was summoned to the court at Pontefract to convict Thomas of Lancaster, who was executed in 1322.

On being granted the manor of Kirby, on 31 August 1319, the Augustinian priory was endowed by Sir Roger de Beler; among the witnesses and a financial supporter of the priory was Sir John Hamelin of Wymondham. On Sir Roger's death in battle, Sir John was appointed by the king to arrest the 'murderers' after the battle at Rearsby.

In the 1790s this engraving of an alabaster effigy of Sir Roger de Beler was published. It has become badly worn and damaged over the centuries (see opposite, lower picture). After Sir Roger de Beler's death in 1326 his widow Alicia Beler held the manor of Kirby. She named the church and village Kirby Belers after her husband. When she died in 1344 her son, Roger de Beler, buried his mother next to his father and erected alabaster effigies over their tomb. In the eighteenth century Belers was changed to Bellars.

The church of St Peter, Kirby Bellars. This engraving was published on 22 October 1790. This church was built from local ironstone in about 1316, possibly at the expense of Sir Roger de Beler. It was extended and rebuilt in part, in the 1400s. Interestingly, in the two nave windows small portions of medieval glass survive.

The tomb of Sir Roger de Beler in the church of St Peter, June 2003.

The tomb of Alicia, the widow of Sir Roger, June 2003.

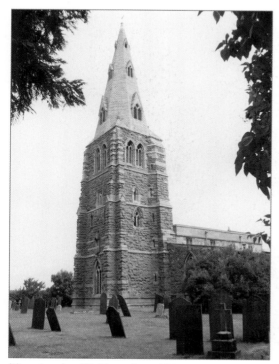

The church of St Peter, June 2003.

The remains of the medieval market cross in front of the church of St Peter, June 2003.

ASHBY FOLVILLE

An engraving of the church of St Mary, Ashby Folville, published in 1790.

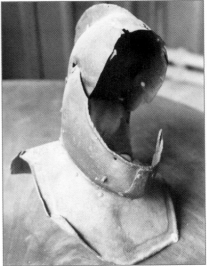

Above: The remains of a helmet that is thought to have belonged to Sir Eustace de Folville, on display in the church of St Mary at Ashby Folville, June 2003.
Left: The tomb of Sir Eustace de Folville, June 2003. The remains of the steel arrow placed in his chest can be viewed, broken and bent, still in position.

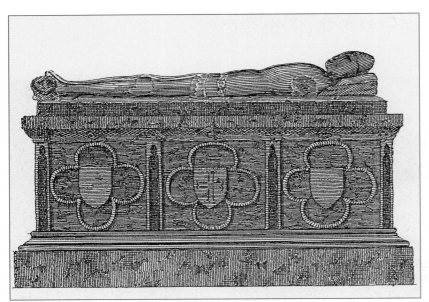

This engraving of the tomb-chest of Sir Eustace de Folville was published in 1790. In 1790 the effigy of this knight had been badly damaged. It is on record that after this monument in the south chapel was erected persons unknown drilled his stone chest and inserted an iron arrow. Eustace was the 'murderer' of Sir Roger de Beler, who endowed the nearby Augustinian priory.

The church of St Mary, Ashby Folville, June 2003. Internal evidence points to the fact that the church was built during the late thirteenth century. Considerable alteration to the internal and external fabric has taken place, and there is a mixture of decorated and Perpendicular architecture.

CIVIL WAR: KIRBY BELLARS

This narrow bridge on the minor road from Kirby Bellars to Asfordby crosses the River Wreake, 1991. Traffic passing over the bridge is controlled by a set of lights. Remains of the original packhorse bridge that served this highway have been incorporated into the present structure. Three arches remain, but four cutwaters are to be seen on the lee side, which indicates there may originally have been more. Underneath the bridge the end of a curved cutwater is clearly visible. Originally built of local granite, the bridge is now a hotch-potch of stone and brick from the eighteenth, nineteenth and twentieth centuries.

Neolithic and Bronze Age man lived in this area, and tumuli or long-forgotten burial sites are still a feature of the landscape. A trade route linked this settlement with other occupation sites in the district and the Romans settled here, building extensive villas in the surrounding countryside. It is doubtful that any of these early settlers found a need to build a bridge across the Wreake at this point. The bed of the river runs across vast deposits of compacted glacial gravel, which provides an ideal place to construct a ford in the shallow river basin. Danes and Saxons lived and possibly fought here, and the Normans, on conquering the district, rebuilt the Saxon church. In August 1319 Roger de Beler, assisted by his mother, Alice (the widow of the founder of Kirby Wrehech) set up a house of Augustinian priests. In 1360 it became a fully fledged priory when canons regular were introduced. This became a powerful institution in medieval times, administering lands throughout the East Midlands. As it was a centre for local trade, it is possible that the packhorse bridge over the Wreake was built on the instructions of the prior of Kirby Bellars sometime towards the end of the fourteenth century. Henry VIII dissolved the priory in 1536 and the responsibility of maintaining the bridge passed into other hands.

With the canalisation of the Wreake in 1797 this bridge was altered considerably. It has subsequently been maintained by the canal and highway authorities without consideration for its historic past, and has suffered badly through neglect.

On 25 February 1645 a troop of fifty Royalist cavalry, under the command of Sir Marmaduke Langdale, rode over the packhorse bridge and engaged a detachment of Parliamentarian cavalry under the command of Captain (later Colonel) Hacker where he had retreated after the battle at Melton Mowbray. In the resulting skirmish the mansion house, which had been captured by the Parliamentarians, was badly damaged by fire. Hacker was routed and fled back to Leicester. He returned later from Leicester and regained control of the remains of the house.

Sir Erasmus de la Fountaine lived in the mansion house, built on the site of the priory, in the middle of the seventeenth century. On 11 June 1642 he was named in the Commission of Array, addressed to Leicestershire by Charles I, and attended the farce at Horse Fair Lees in Leicester when a shower of rain dampened both the powder and the ardour of the protagonists (see pp. 28–30). This did not go down well with the Parliamentarians. By 7 December 1643 the Royalist commander-in-chief, Hastings from Ashby de la Zouch, had installed a troop of cavalry at Kirby Bellars to control the Leicester to Nottingham road through Melton Mowbray. This mansion house changed hands during a number of skirmishes during the English Civil War. The photograph dates from 1994.

MELTON MOWBRAY

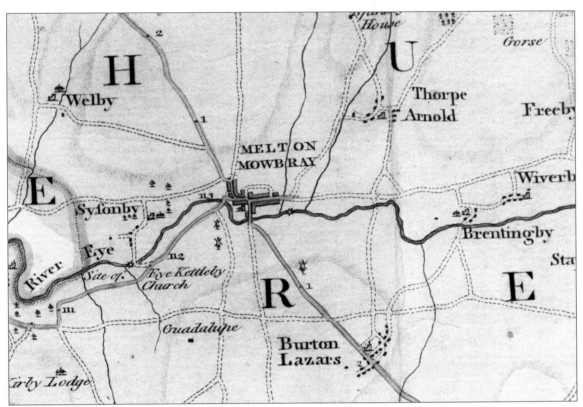

This is part of an interesting map of Melton Mowbray published in 1777 by John Prior. Melton Mowbray is nothing more than a large village on a junction on a number of important roads. All the properties are situated north of the River Eye/Wreake. What is important is the position of the three windmills to the south of the town. If they existed in the 1640s the Parliamentarians would have used them as observation towers. Just under a thousand Parliamentary troops advanced, possibly along the roads from Thorpe Arnold and Brentingby, to join the troops already situated in the town. Langdale's cavalry marched in from Burton Lazars and Great Dalby.

A panoramic view of Melton Mowbray, drawn by William Latham in 1871, showing the site of the famous battle at Melton Mowbray in the Civil War on 25 February 1645. During the war there was considerable passage of arms in and around this town. In 1643 a vicious confrontation took place at Waltham-on-the-Wolds, and on 21 September some Parliamentarian troops were badly beaten up at Long Clawson by troops from Belvoir Castle.

Royalists held strong defensive positions at the castles at Ashby de la Zouch and Belvoir and in 1643 were gaining control of the countryside in the north of Leicestershire. Gervase Lucas was appointed colonel by the king for his success in capturing Belvoir Castle for the Royalists. On 25 September 1643 Lucas was instructed to remove the nest of rebels that resided at Melton Mowbray. That prevented movement of Royalist troops through this important road junction to Belvoir and Newark. The governor of Newark provided a troop of 300 horses and dragoons. At about midnight on 27 September the combined forces from Newark and Belvoir Castle assembled outside the town and under the direction of Colonel Lucas, surprised all the Parliamentarians in their beds, at about 3 a.m. Only one officer refused to surrender and he was run through on the spot. The Royalists took 16 officers prisoner and about 300 soldiers, over 300 horses and an enormous quantity of arms. Captain Francis Hacker of Colston Bassett was taken prisoner and escorted to Belvoir by his brother, Rowland, a captain of foot in Charles I's army. Arthur Staveley of Melton Mowbray and Thomas Hesilrige of Noseley were also taken prisoner, but they had obtained their release by November.

In January 1645 the king was making his last attempt to win a major battle and achieve a suitable compromise. He instructed the fine professional soldier Sir Marmaduke Langdale to survey north-east Leicestershire. He charged through Market Harborough, Melton Mowbray and on to Belvoir Castle, brushing aside any Parliamentarian opposition. On 24 February 1645 Langdale, with an army of some 3,000 troops, mainly cavalry, marched north from Oxford to clear the roadway to Newark. Colonel Edward Rossiter of Grantham and Captain Francis Hacker of Kirby Bellars were informed of this advancing army. Rossiter approached Melton Mowbray through Waltham-on-the-Wolds and Buckminster with approximately 2,000 mounted cavalry. He was warned of Langdale's cavalry approaching the town and made the terrible mistake of charging up hill out of the town towards Great Dalby, on what is now Dalby Road and Ankle Hill. The horses were winded, Hacker only half-heartedly attacked the rear and the result was inevitable.

The Parliamentarians were cut down as they reached the top of the hill in the first charge; they retreated and charged again. Outnumbered, many were killed and the Roundheads fled the field. Langdale then advanced towards Kirby Bellars to take on the fleeing Parliamentarians, but they set fire to the manor house and fled back to Leicester. On assessment approximately thirty Royalists were killed. The victorious Cavaliers marched on to Belvoir Castle where at least two officers died of their wounds. On the morning of 26 February just over 100 naked corpses lay in the fields and at the fords across the river. Locals had robbed the dead. In the watermeadows, the bodies of the dead soldiers were all buried together in an anonymous mass grave.

A view from the fields off Burton Road with the bridge and ford on the left, 1911. The elms are high in the background. It was in these fields that the battle at Melton Mowbray took place in 1645.

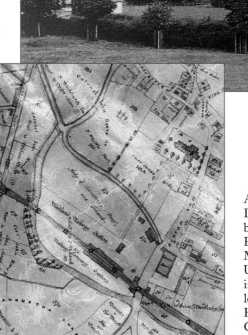

A section of the map drawn by William Latham in 1871. This is the site of the battle that took place between the Parliamentarian occupiers of Melton Mowbray and the attacking Royalists. Unrelated to this battle there are some interesting features: the canal basin; the level crossing across Burton End; Ankle Hill, now Dalby Road; and Sir Francis Grant's home and garden near the railway bridge.

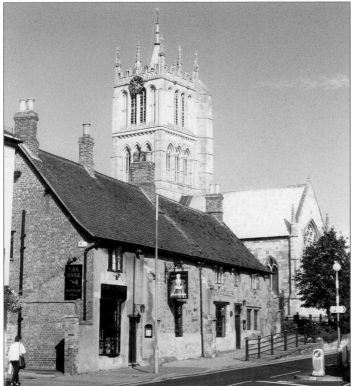

The Bede House on Burton Street, 1904. These almshouses were opened in 1646 as a result of a gift of land and cash in 1638. During the Civil War battle that took place in 1645 these properties were being completed opposite the church of St Mary. Roundheads and Royalists charged up and down the road between the church and the building site opposite.

Anne of Cleves Restaurant, August 2003. This ancient building was possibly used by Parliamentarians when they occupied the town of Melton Mowbray in the 1640s. It would have given them some satisfaction to be occupying a royal house.

A view of Melton Mowbray from the top of Ankle Hill, 1905. At the time of the battle in 1645 no trees or shrubs would have existed on the sloping fields leading down into the town.

The church of St Mary, August 2003. Were observers acting on behalf of the Roundheads situated on the top of this church tower in 1645?

The River Eye and Lady Wilton's Bridge, 1930. On this site in 1645 a ford existed across the river. During the battle, over 100 soldiers were killed, mainly with sword cuts and being run through. Their lifeblood drained away into the river, which was 'ankle deep in blood'.

BURROUGH-ON-THE-HILL

An engraving of the hill at Burrough, showing the Iron Age fortress, published in 1790. Legends abound concerning Burrough-on-the-Hill encampment. Fact and fiction combine; spasmodic archaeological digs since the eighteenth century have produced an incomplete story.

This naturally easily fortified hill was possibly first in use in the Neolithic period. It is a commanding hill of limestone and ironstone, which overlooks the valleys to the south-west, north-west and on over to the Vale of Belvoir in the north. The area was occupied by the Coritani at the time of the Roman occupation. Some early historians consider this the site of a famous battle, where the Iceni were defeated by Ostorius. Certainly the Romans occupied the site. If it was defended by the Coritani there would have been a long siege, on three sides the defended walls would have been impossible to attack successfully. The slopes up to the defensive walls would have been too high. The fortress had religious significance to the occupying Coritani; possibly they would have defended their homes to the last man. The main attack could only proceed along the existing footpath from the present car park on the Somerby to Burrough-on-the-Hill road. Evidence exists that the Romans lived on the site; perhaps they believed it had religious significance. Did the Saxons offer some form of defence during the Danish invasion of this area?

Some nineteenth-century amateur archaeologists thought they had found building blocks of stone, held together with lime mortar. Today all the evidence suggests that this natural site was defended by embankments of packed soil and stone, surmounted by a palisade of sharpened wooden tree trunks, making a strongly constructed fence, with interior wooden walkways to provide an observation post. Attacking troops attempting to climb up to the protective walls would have been easily expelled. A section of John Prior's map of 1777 is printed on p. 179. At the top left-hand corner is featured Burrough-on-the-Hill with a building standing in the centre of the hill.

A plan of the Burrough-on-the-Hill fortifications published in 1907. All major attacks would have come from the south-east in this plan, as an extensive gateway is indicated.

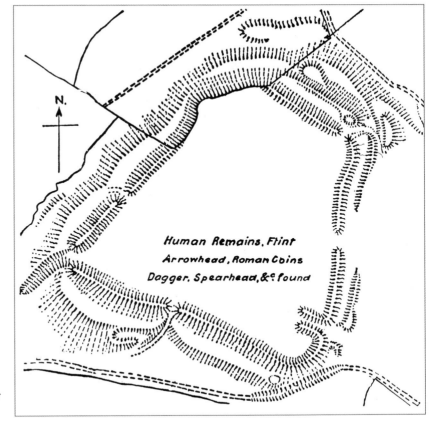

Human Remains, Flint Arrowhead, Roman Coins Dagger, Spearhead, &c. found

Burrough Hill, from the road to Little Dalby, August 2003. For further information consult pp. 103–5 in my *The Best of Leicestershire*, Sutton, 2003.

SAUVEY CASTLE

Sauvey Castle was built during the reign of King John (1199–1216) possibly in the years around 1200. It was financed by the Basset family. Richard Bassett founded the nearby priory of Launde between 1119 and 1125. The castle was erected at the north-west corner of Leighfield Forest. In 1209 King John was at Nottingham Castle on 10 November, Mountsorrel Castle on the 11th, at Trencheland, Sauvey Castle on the 12th, and then at Rockingham Castle on the 13th. Castles such as these four were very important to this king. Similar castles were erected throughout England: without such closely intertwined fortifications he could not have attempted to control his awkward barons. A record exists and states that £442 13s 1d was spent by Hugh de Neville to repair and construct buildings inside the castle walls and clean out the fishponds in 1211.

After signing the Magna Carta in 1215 King John proceeded to suppress his barons further. In his northern campaign of 1215–16 he attempted to secure the line of the Great North Road to Lincoln and beyond. He laid siege to Belvoir Castle, ordering the constables of Belvoir and Sauvey to extract taxes from the surrounding countryside, and eventually sacking the castle at Belvoir. John had appointed William de Huntinfield as governor of Sauvey Castle, but in 1215 Huntinfield joined the rebels and was removed by force of arms by the end of the year. John then appointed Hugh de Neville to look after his interests in Leighfield Forest. This appointment did not last very long, and John appointed William de Fortibus, the 2nd Earl of Albemarle, as governor of the castle.

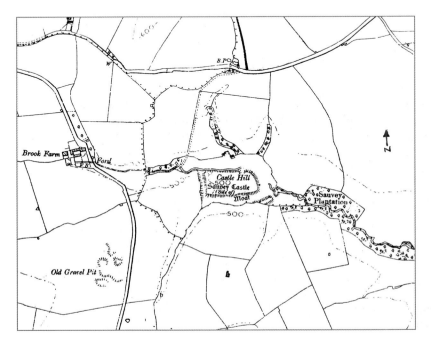

An extract from a plan of Owston and Withcote estates in 1926. This plan was based on the current Ordnance Survey. The castle site stands south of the Halstead to Knossington crossroads, below Owston woods.

This engraving, by Goldar, was produced from King John's features carved on his tomb at Worcester, and was published on 7 April 1787.

On the death of John in 1216 he was succeeded by his nine-year-old son, Henry III. During his minority, the young king re-enacted the Magna Carta with a group of barons who nominated the king's regent as William Marshall, Earl of Pembroke. The regent, on instructions from his king, ordered that the 2nd Earl of Albemarle should retain his position as governor of Sauvey Castle. In 1216 the troops that had been recruited in and around Sauvey Castle and Leighfield were ordered under the arms of the Earl of Albemarle to march on Whitwick Castle, to place it under siege and to remove the governor, Saer de Quincy. After a short siege the castle capitulated. The regent took control. Possibly the Earl of Pembroke requested that after the Battle of Lincoln, Mountsorrel Castle should be controlled by an appointed constable from Sauvey. The Earl of Pembroke instigated regional control in districts such as this area of the Midlands. It did not work because the local barons proceeded to act as individuals, raising their own taxes with little or no respect for the young king and his regent. The two central Midlands castles, Rockingham and Sauvey, certainly objected. William de Forz, Earl of Aumale, a rebellious baron, rejected the king's wishes. While travelling north in 1219 the young Henry III was actually denied access to Rockingham Castle. His troops were too small in number to lay siege and they certainly could not travel through Leighfield Forest to Sauvey. A large army was formed by the regent and in the king's name his troops laid siege to the two castles. On 23 June 1220 both castles surrendered and Sauvey was placed in the hands of Stephen de Segrave to hold in the king's name. He held the castle for five years. In 1220 the manor of Withcote came under the control of the abbot of Owston and the prior of Laund. It is interesting to guess how this affected the baronial wars in this area. The church expected their taxes, and the barons were certainly involved in plunder. The baronial wars continued to such a degree that life had little or no value to the local population. The king was trying to provide stability for his people with considerable difficulty. By 1244 Gilbert de Segrave was the justice of the forest. Now called the Royal Forest of Leicestershire and Rutland, the Forest of Leighfield stretched from Rockingham through Rutland into Leicestershire, along the border of the two counties below Oakham.

Certainly this castle took part in the baronial wars of the 1260s, and it was undoubtedly a burden to Henry III. Sauvey Castle was placed under the direct defence for the king. John de Plesetis, Earl of Warwick, took control of the castle, when William Baged was ordered to surrender the counties of Warwickshire and Leicestershire. In 1264, under the leadership of Simon de Montfort, the barons rebelled and defeated the king's army at Lewes. The weak king was taken prisoner.

For one year, effectively, the country was ruled by Simon de Montfort, who led one group of barons, through a council of fifteen magnates backed by a national assembly: England's first Parliament. The barons split into two factions, one group under de Montfort, the other backing the king and his son. This resulted in the Battle of Evesham where Simon de Montfort was killed. The upshot was that for the last few years of Henry III's life, his son Edward ruled the country.

In 1272 Edward I became king. He was very unlike Henry. His word was law; he expanded the first Parliament. Edward's far-reaching legal administration resulted in the baronial castles such as Sauvey being no longer needed. By 1289 Sauvey Castle was in disrepair, pillaged for lead and stone.

Sauvey had been built to control the royal forest stretching from Rockingham Castle in the east to Sauvey Castle in the west. It was erected on the edge of the forest, partly also to keep charge of the local populace. It linked with the other castles in the Midlands. It stood on a tip of land jutting out from the woodland, where small streams fed on excellent supplies of water, enabling fishponds and the moat to be constructed.

There are many unanswered questions on the building and the demolition of Sauvey Castle. It stood on a remote site, not easily accessible to the public. Eventually a controlled archaeological excavation will take place, and then this castle will take its correct place in the history of England.

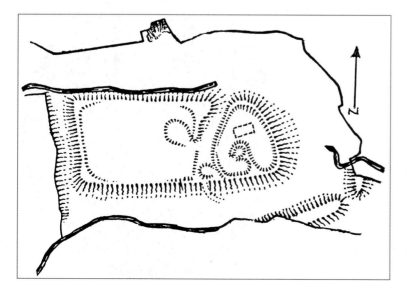

An enlarged version of the smaller plan of Sauvey Castle on p. 176. This indicates the moat created by damming the tributary of the River Chater. It also clearly illustrates a ring motte and bailey. Inside the defensive walls there is a hall, a kitchen block and domestic apartments, as well as a chapel, constructed in 1244.

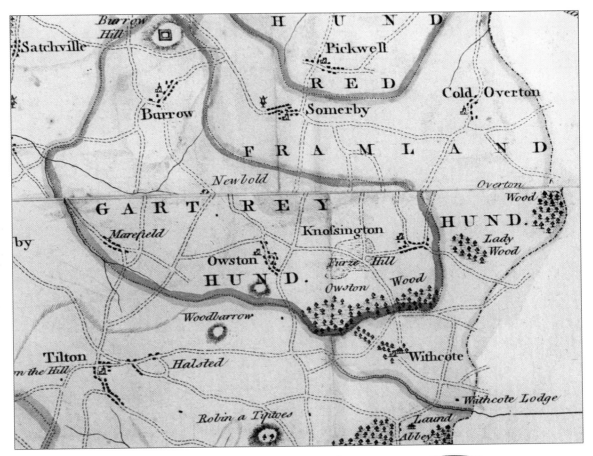

A section of John Prior's map of 1777. There is no indication of a castle near Withcote Hall. It is interesting to note that buildings are standing in the centre of the fortifications at Burrow Hill (Burrough on the Hill) (see p. 174).

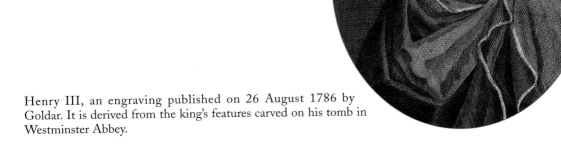

Henry III, an engraving published on 26 August 1786 by Goldar. It is derived from the king's features carved on his tomb in Westminster Abbey.

Michael Mason at the entrance to the footpath leading from the Leicester to Oakham road opposite Owston woods, June 2003. This footpath passes along the edge of the western perimeter of Sauvey Castle.

The south-west corner of the moat, 1970s. This ditch would have been excavated to construct the moat and build the protective walls.

Fallen stones that have collected
at the base of the castle wall along
the north face of the defences,
June 2003.

Withcote Hall, an engraving by J. Cary from a drawing by J. Pridden, 11 July 1793. The hall was the home
of the Revd Henry Smith; the Smith family may have become lords of the manor in the fifteenth century.
The first hall was probably built after Sauvey Castle served no further purpose and the magnificent collection
of stone became available. In the existing hall evidence has survived of the original house. Most of the building
on the present site was built in 1723, and was completely restored in 1856.

HALLATON

The conical market cross on the village green in Hallaton, opposite the Bewicke Arms, July 2003. In this village the renowned Hallaton Hare Pie Scramble and Bottle-kicking event takes place at Easter. Pagan sacrifices occurred on hilltops at this village in the early years of Saxon domination, before Christianity evolved on religious sites. There was particular emphasis on the hare.

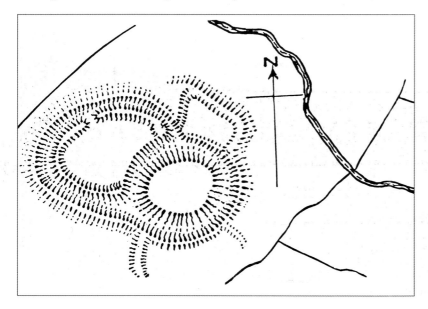

This plan of Hallaton Castle was published in 1907. It shows a typical Norman motte and bailey defensive structure. Romans occupied hilltops in the area, and earlier Iron Age mining took place. Alctone (Hallaton) was granted to Geoffrey of Alselin in 1066 and he held this district at the time of the Domesday survey. On the death of William I in 1100 his young bastard son, William Peverel, obtained various estates throughout the Midlands. It is fairly certain he built this castle to protect his interest in the open-cast mining of iron ore.

Hallaton Castle in 1790. During the reign of Stephen, William Peverel supported the king in his battle against the Scots in 1138. In the wars against the barons in the following years, it is fairly certain he repelled numerous attacks on this castle. In 1140 in the Battle of Lincoln he was captured and held prisoner on the instructions of Empress Maud. Possibly as early as this, a castle in such an isolated area lost its importance because the iron ore had been worked out, by providing material for swords and armour in this turbulent period of English history.

Good footpath access is available to walk to this castle site. Footpath markers are indicated to the west of the church of St Michael and All Angels. From the footpath the castle is visible in the background of this photograph of July 2003.

Don Humberston standing in the defensive ditch below the motte at Hallaton Castle, July 2003.

MEDBOURNE

This picturesque bridge straddles the Medbourne Brook near the church of St Giles in a village steeped in history. The brook rises in Cranoe, Tugby, Hallaton and Horninghold, and feeds into the River Welland just south of the village. Medbourne parish is on the line of a Bronze Age road, obviously connected with the iron-ore excavations of nearby Hallaton. Celtic remains have been found near the village.

A large Roman villa was excavated in the late eighteenth century and it is presumed that the village was built on the site of a Roman army encampment. The Saxons occupied the site; their pottery and bronze artefacts have been uncovered in this area for many years. It is hardly likely that a bridge was built over the brook by the early settlers, as it would have been easily fordable for most of the year. The brook curves around the west perimeter of the churchyard.

A moat was constructed to defend, possibly, a building of religious significance in the early years of the Norman Conquest. This moat encircles the church, on the site of an early construction during the reign of Stephen, which was an age of anarchy when the church would have been a haven from the marauding bands of lawless mercenaries in the pay of local barons. A bridge to the church would have been needed, possibly across the west side, over Medbourne Brook, but it would have been a drawbridge, not a permanent structure. After the death of Stephen a new era began, and ecclesiastical control was extended. In 1262 the manor of Medbourne was granted by Henry III to William Chaudeler, passing to John de Kirby, who was Bishop of Ely at his death in 1290. It is believed that the present bridge was constructed during this period.

The packhorse bridge leading to the church of St Giles, July 2003.

Inside the defensive moat leading to the packhorse bridge, July 2003.

A view of the packhorse bridge at Medbourne, 1993. On Friday 3 April 1646 this site was the scene of a desperate battle between the villagers and an organised troop of Parliamentarian soldiers. The parson had arrested one of the troop and held him in the church. It is thought the Medbourne Brook had been dammed, so filling the moat with water, to form a defendable island.

Medbourne has had a turbulent past. One of the most unsettled times was at the end of the Civil War. Leicester was re-taken by Parliamentarian forces on 16 June 1645, and after this engagement and the decisive Battle of Naseby two days before, bands of undisciplined troops roamed the Leicestershire countryside. The situation was not improved by the Parliamentarian bureaucrats denying pay to their victorious soldiers. Troops were camped around the Midlands and one such contingent was billeted at Caldecott, outside Rockingham Castle. Ten troopers from this company were on a foraging mission when they arrived at Medbourne on 3 April 1646, seeking food and horses and bent on plunder, if the villagers could not prove their loyalty to Parliament. They sought out the village constable but he was absent, and the local parson took exception to the attitude of the Roundheads and had one

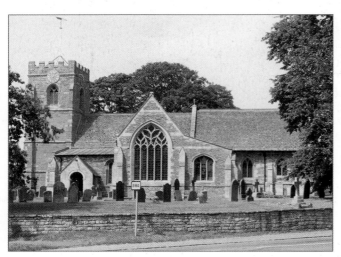

The church of St Giles, July 2003.

arrested. This incensed the rest, who started a fight. By this time, the entire village was alerted and a general fracas ensued, the villagers being armed with pitchforks, hoes, hedge knives and some guns. The battle was centred on and around the bridge and moated churchyard. Through force of numbers, the villagers gained the upper hand and the professionals retreated, fighting a rearguard action, and driving cattle with them as protective cover. They made a stand in drays on a field about a mile away from the village. Unbeknown to the villagers one trooper had ridden off to alert a further troop of twenty cavalrymen who were foraging about a quarter of a mile away near Holt. They charged into the fight giving the untrained villagers no quarter; the parson's servant received a sword slash that 'had his bowels let out with wound' and many others had their hands cut off defending themselves. By this time the constable, James Barret, returned and tried to stop the conflict. He was run through with the swords of five troopers for his trouble. After looting and pillaging the village the soldiers drove the stolen cattle away with them. This atrocity was not ignored and a party of Leicester horse and dragoons were sent into Rutland to apprehend the culprits. Most of them were part of Major Thomas Babbington of Rothley's company of horse. When they returned to the main camp at Lydington with their 'spoils of war' they were arrested and taken back to Leicester Gaol to await their trial. It is not known whether this trial ever took place.

MARKET HARBOROUGH

Market Harborough from the south, featuring a packhorse bridge with a ford across the River Welland, 1792. A carrier's cart is travelling into the town. On 8 September 1642 one of the first major encounters of the Civil War took place in Market Harborough. Prince Rupert had over 2,000 cavalry quartered in villages in and around the town. He was made aware of the fact that the Parliamentarians were storing hay for horses and quantities of supplies in the town. In the evening of the 8th he entered the town with 1,000 cavalry and a small number of troops. Several houses were plundered, hay was loaded on carts, many arms were taken and horses formed into groups to be led away. Unfortunately for Rupert, he did not make the perimeter of the town secure. Unbeknown to Rupert, a Parliamentarian soldier slipped away to the Earl of Stamford who was camped a short distance away with 800 cavalry and many foot soldiers. Spending the night in the town, and no doubt consuming too much wine, they set out towards Leicester and Melton Mowbray. Stamford laid an ambush on Galley Hill, under cover of a spinney of conifers. This was well planned, and Rupert's cavalry and troops met a frontal attack from Parliamentarian troops who had remained well hidden, along with men from the town who wanted to retrieve their property, from the rear. The surprise was complete. Thirty of Rupert's foot soldiers were killed on the spot. Rupert turned about and attempted to return to occupy the town. Houses on both sides of the highway were now well defended by Parliamentarians. Rupert fought his way though the town, crossing the ford indicated in the engraving above. He only succeeded in saving the mounted cavalry, and lost all the booty and all of his foot soldiers, who were either killed or captured. He fled eastward to the security of Rockingham Castle.

Smith Charity School, one of the properties that was occupied by Parliamentarian forces during the 1642 skirmish in Market Harborough, opened in 1614. The prosperous town was well disposed to the government, to the defence of the Protestant religion, and to the liberty of the subject. This photograph dates from the 1920s.

The Market Square, Market Harborough, 1905. Though it was a Parliamentarian town at the height of the English Civil War, Royalists controlled much of the countryside around it and cavalry rode through this square on numerous occasions. Did Roundheads set up an observation point in the tower of the Church of Dionysius? In January 1645 Royalist troops under Sir Marmaduke Langdale charged through the town on their way to Melton Mowbray, and in February over 3,000 Royalists subdued the town. Some Royalists probably arrived in this market square before the fierce battle just over the county border at Naseby. Rupert occupied the town on Friday 13 June 1645. After the Royalist defeat 700 were killed on the battlefield, 400 between Market Harborough and Leicester, and 500 were taken prisoner at Market Harborough. The records show that 170 Roundheads were killed.

KING GEORGE VI

HRH Prince Albert wearing Royal Air Force uniform, c. 1920. He was eighteen when the First World War broke out in 1914. He joined the navy and went to sea, and was a serving officer at the Battle of Jutland. He became one of the first officers in the new fighting force, the Royal Air Force.

In 1936 he became king after his elder brother abdicated. In 1939 the Second World War commenced. Great Britain stood alone facing the greatest menace ever to threaten the country in 1940. The king with his devoted queen and two children remained resolute and courageous at his post of danger and duty. If he had been a medieval king he would have led his troops into battle, regardless of his fate. In 1946 George VI ordained that the Leicestershire Regiment should become the Royal Leicestershire Regiment in recognition of its outstanding achievements. He visited Leicester personally to make the award.

Bibliography

Dictionary of British Kings and Queens, 1995

Leicestershire and Rutland Magazine, 1948–50

Bonser, R., *Aviation in Leicestershire and Rutland*, 2001

Bryant, A., *1000 Years of British Monarchy*, 1973

Cartwright, T.C., *Bird's Eye Wartime Leicestershire 1939–1945*, 2002

Dryden, A. (ed.), *Memorials of Old Leicestershire*, 1911

Ellison, P., *The Owston and Withcote Estates*, 1926

Foss, P., *Sauvey Castle, Leicestershire: Sycamore Leaves*, 1983

Fox, A.W., *Kirby Bellars: A Parish History*, 1997

Fox, L., *Leicester Castle*, 1944

Gretton, J., *Stapleford Park*, 1958

Griel, M. and Dressel, J., *Zeppelin: The German Airship Story*, 1990

Harvey, D., *Monuments to Courage*, Vol. I, 1999

Hickman, T., *The History of Stilton Cheese*, 2001

Hilliam, D., *Kings, Queens, Bones and Bastards*, 2003

Kelly, W., *Royal Progresses and Visits to Leicester*, 1884

Kemp, R.A., *The History of the Olde Trip to Jerusalem*, 1994

Morris, J. (ed.), *Domesday Book 1086: Leicestershire*, 1979

Nichols, J., *The History and Antiquities of the County of Leicester* (4 vols), 1795–1811

Page, W. (ed.), *The Victoria History of the County of Leicester*, Vol. I, 1907

Pevsner, N., *Leicestershire and Rutland*, 1984

Pridham, C.H.B., *Lewis Gun*, 1944

Rimell, L.R., *The Airship V.C.*, 1989

Roberson, J.N. and Tallis, J.G., *The History of RAF Cottesmore*, 1991

Salter, M., *The Castles of the East Midlands*, 2002

Scaysbrook, P.H., *The Civil War in Leicestershire and Rutland*, 1993

Skillington, S.H., *The Newarke*, 1912

Symonds, R., *Marches of the Royal Army*, 1859

Tanks, E., *The Ironstone Quarries of the Midlands: Rutland*, 1989

Tew, D., *The Oakham Canal*, 1968

Belgrave Mill, *c.* 1790. In the Royalist attack on Leicester in 1645, Sir H. Baird's troops occupied this mill as an advance position, outside the walls of the town. It was demolished in the 1890s.

Acknowledgements

For very many years I have been interested in the battlefield sites of Leicestershire. Certainly one major battle, the Battle of Bosworth Field, changed the course of English history. As important as this event was, there were many other major incidents and skirmishes that not only affected the lives of ordinary people living in the county, but also made an impact on national affairs. This book is a record from the past; visual assessments and research are only possible with the help of other interested individuals. The author's grateful thanks are extended to: Jo and Don Humberston; Mary and Terry Toms; Squire de Lisle; Mark Bowen; Lady Gretton; Michael Mason and the author's grandchildren, who expressed a keen interest in exploring battlefield sites.

All the historic images are out of copyright, the author holds the originals in his personal collection. The author retains copyright of all the other photographs. The author records his thanks for all the work that Jenny Weston has put in, processing the manuscript for presentation to Sutton Publishing.

Ashby de la Zouch Castle, *c.* 1730.

Index of Selected Battle Sites & Participants